WITHDRAWN

THE CITY IN ANCIENT ISRAEL

THE CITY
IN ANCIENT ISRAEL

Volkmar Fritz

Sheffield Academic Press

To my wife
Anke

Copyright © 1995 Sheffield Academic Press

Published by
Sheffield Academic Press Ltd
Mansion House
19 Kingfield Road
Sheffield, S11 9AS
England

Typeset by Sheffield Academic Press
and
Printed on acid-free paper in Great Britain
by The Cromwell Press
Melksham, Wiltshire

British Library Cataloguing in Publication Data

A catalogue record for this book is available
from the British Library

ISBN 1-85075-477-2

CONTENTS

ABBREVIATIONS

AASOR	The Annual of the American Schools of Oriental Research
AJA	*American Journal of Archaeology*
ANET	J.B. Pritchard (ed.), *Ancient Near Eastern Texts*
AOAT	Alter Orient und Altes Testament
BA	*Biblical Archaeologist*
BARev	*Biblical Archaeology Review*
BASOR	*Bulletin of the American Schools of Oriental Research*
Bib	*Biblica*
BN	*Biblische Notizen*
BRL	Biblisches Reallexikon, ed. K. Galling,[2] 1977
BWANT	Beiträge zur Wissenschaft des Alten und Neuen Testaments
BZAW	Beihefte zur *ZAW*
EA	J.A. Knudtzon, Die El-Amarna-Tafeln, 1907-15
EvT	*Evangelische Theologie*
FRLANT	Forschungen zur Religion und Literatur des Alten und Neuen Testaments
HTR	*Harvard Theological Review*
IEJ	*Israel Exploration Journal*
JAOS	*Journal of the American Oriental Society*
JBL	*Journal of Biblical Literature*
JEA	*Journal of Egyptian Archaeology*
JNES	*Journal of Near Eastern Studies*
MDOG	*Mitteilungen der Deutschen Orient-Gesellschaft*
NEAEHL	*The New Encyclopedia of Archaeological Excavations in the Holy Land*
PEFQSt	*Palestine Exploration Fund, Quarterly Statement*
PEQ	*Palestine Exploration Quarterly*
PJ	*Palästina-Jahrbuch*
RLA	*Reallexikon der Assyriologie und Vorderasiatischen Archäologie*
SAM	Sheffield Archaeological Monographs
TLZ	*Theologische Literaturzeitung*
UF	*Ugarit Forschungen*
VT	*Vetus Testamentum*
WMANT	Wissenschaftliche Monographien zum Alten und Neuen Testament

ZAW   Zeitschrift für die alttestamentliche Wissenschaft
ZDPV   Zeitschrift des deutschen Palästina-Vereins
ZTK   Zeitschrift für Theologie und Kirche

LIST OF FIGURES

Chapter 1

CITY AND STATE IN ANCIENT ISRAEL

The first reference to Israel is found on the victory stele of Merenptah (1224–1204).[1] In addition to Canaan and other lands, the name Israel is expressly applied to a people numbered among the enemies conquered by this Pharaoh; the area settled by this people cannot, however, be more closely identified.[2] In the Bible, Israel occurs as the name used of themselves by a people who have formed an association of tribes. The beginnings of this consolidation are just as unknown as the origin of the name, since its possible translation as 'El rules' provides no information about the original use of the term. The oldest biblical text—the Song of Deborah in Judges 5—mentions ten tribes which had allied together under this name in the eleventh century BC;[3] their alliance has its foundations in a common history of settlement and in their veneration of the same God, Yahweh.[4]

1. The stele was found in Thebes and is now in the Cairo Museum. A new translation of the whole text is offered by E. Hornung, 'Die Israelstele des Merneptah', in *Fontes atque Pontes: Eine Festgabe für Hellmut Brunner* (1983), pp. 224-33. For the history of research cf. H. Engel, 'Die Siegesstele des Merenptah. Kritischer Überblick über die verschiedenen Versuche historischer Auswertung des Schlußabschnittes', *Bib* 60 (1979), pp. 373-99. The problem of whether this Pharaoh undertook a campaign in Palestine does not need to be discussed in this context.

2. This unambiguous fact has been contested in G.W. Ahlström, *Who Were the Israelites?* (1986), pp. 37-43.

3. For an understanding of the song in Judges 5 cf. A. Weiser, 'Das Deborahlied- eine gattungs- und traditionsgeschichtliche Studie', *ZAW* 71 (1959), pp. 67-97; H.-P. Müller, 'Der Aufbau des Deborahliedes', *VT* 16 (1966), pp. 446-59; J.A. Soggin, 'Bemerkungen zum Deborahlied, Richter Kap.5', *TLZ* 106 (1981), pp. 625-39.

4. The origin of the worship of Jahweh is obscure, since the constitutive monotheism in the Israelite religion only first prevailed during the course of the period of the monarchy; cf. S. Herrmann, 'Der alttestamentliche Gottesname', in *Gesammelte*

Only theoretical suppositions can be put forward concerning the origin of the Israelite tribes and their acquisition of territory in which to live, since there are no sources in existence which are useful from a historical point of view.[5] The Book of Joshua, with its account of the conquest and division of the land, is excluded as a historical record since this is a fictitious representation which was only written several centuries after the acquisition of the land. It is probable that the early Israelites were nomads who kept and raised animals; their existence was closely bound up with the cultivable land and after 1200, they gradually changed over to permanent settlement.[6] The reason for the acquisition of permanent places of domicile could have been that, with the downfall of the Canaanite cities, the centuries-old symbiosis that had existed between the Late Bronze Age city-states and the nomadic peoples in their vicinity had broken down.[7]

Also the accounts found in the Book of Judges do not provide information about the period between the permanent settlement of the Israelite tribes and the formation of the state under Saul around 1025. It is not possible to deduce any more from these traditions than the fact that the individual tribes carried on their own lives to a broad degree, and only undertook joint action in the case of war, which they either carried on against one individual tribe or against an external enemy. Amongst these enemies were not only the autochthonous population of Palestine in the last remaining centres, but also the neighbouring peoples such as the Philistines of the southern coastal plain, the Ammonites, Moabites and Edomites of the Transjordan[8] who had also taken over their new area of settlement after 1200, and the Midianites, who pushed forward into the area of cultivable land as camel-riding nomads from the Arabian desert. Although the regions settled by the individual tribes have been

Studien zur Geschichte des Alten Testaments (1986), pp. 76-88; M. Görg, 'Anfänge israelitischen Gottesglaubens', *Kairos* 18 (1976), pp. 256-64; E.A. Knauf, *Midian* (1988), pp. 43-63.

5.   Cf. the research report by M. Weippert, *Die Landnahme der israelitischen Stämme in der neueren wissenschaftlichen Diskussion* (FRLANT 92; 1967).

6.   A. Alt, *Die Landnahme der Israeliten in Palästina und Erwägungen über die Landnahme der Israeliten in Palästina. Kleine Schriften zur Geschichte des Volkes Israel*, I (1953), pp. 89-125 and 126-75.

7.   Cf. V. Fritz, 'Conquest or Settlement? The Early Iron Age in Palestine', *BA* 50 (1987), pp. 84-100.

8.   Cf. U. Hübner, *Die Ammoniter* (ADPV 16; 1992); P. Bienkowski (ed.), *Early Edom and Moab* (SAM 7; 1992).

identified, exact definition of the limits of these areas is not possible since occasional shifting of borders took place during the premonarchical period.[9]

Particularly in the mountain areas, but also in the various plains and in the Negev, numerous newly-established villages have been identified which were situated outside the area of the former city-states and only in exceptional cases exceeded half to one hectare (c. 1.25-2.5 acres) in area.[10] Occasionally, these villages only consisted of a few houses, but there were also large villages with about two hundred house units. As a rule they were unfortified, but a defensive position could be achieved through a circular arrangement of the houses. In their layout, these agricultural settlements differed markedly from one another and from the few Canaanite cities which were still in existence and had survived the destruction of the city-states in the twelfth century. A number of these settlements were only inhabited for a short time, and this form of settlement was completely abandoned at the beginning of the monarchy (cf. below, Chapter 4).

With the establishment of the monarchy a state developed out of the alliance between the tribes,[11] and the name Israel now denoted all of the tribes together except for Judah. Consequently the name Israel, after the death of Solomon, applied to the northern kingdom as opposed to the southern kingdom of Judah. The monarchy brought far-reaching changes for the people, including forms of urban settlement which were new for Israel. The new form of the state necessitated the new establishment of cities on various grounds:

1.　The city reflected the new self-confidence of the state.
2.　It was only by means of fortified cities that the country could be defended against external enemies.

9.　On the area settled by individual tribes cf. K.-D. Schunck, *Benjamin* (BZAW 86; 1963); H.M. Niemann, *Die Daniten* (FRLANT 132; 1985). On the lists concerned with tribal geography cf. M. Noth, 'Studien zu den historisch-geographischen Dokumenten des Josua-Buches', *ZDPV* 58 (1935), pp. 185-255 = *Aufsätze zur biblischen Landes- und Altertumskunde*, I (1971), pp. 229-80; Y. Aharoni, *The Land of the Bible* (2nd edn, 1979), pp. 248-62; Z. Kallai, *Historical Geography of the Bible* (1986).

10.　Cf. the summary of research to date in I. Finkelstein, *The Archaeology of the Israelite Settlement* (1988).

11.　Cf. here A. Alt, *Die Staatenbildung der Israeliten in Palästina, Kleine Schriften zur Geschichte des Volkes Israel*, II (1953), pp. 1-65; F. Crüsemann, *Der Widerstand gegen das Königtum* (WMANT 32; 1978).

3. The administration of the kingdom depended upon institutions which could best function from within the cities.
4. The recognizable growth in the population could be accommodated within the newly-founded cities.

Thus the process of urbanization which had its new beginnings around the year 1000 is the result of a political change, and not the consequence of a social development. The establishment of cities in Ancient Israel is an expression of a political will and not a consequence of the continuation of an existing form of settlement. Leaving aside the fact that the city has a long history in Palestine, the urbanization during the period of the monarchy represents a new beginning, in which older elements are incorporated but have a completely new concept and new building forms as their vehicle.

The reasons for the establishment of the monarchy in Israel are for the most part obscure. Certainly the pressure exerted by the Philistines on the tribes of the mountain range of central Palestine was decisive. In order to create a central authority Saul was named the first king by the people, since it was only under a strong leadership that the threat from the Philistine city-states could be met. The extent of the region under the authority of Saul is as little documented as is the length of his reign. There are, however, good grounds for the assumption that he ruled over all the tribes west and east of the Jordan and that his reign lasted from about 1025 to 1004.

Saul's successor, David, then became King of Judah in Hebron in 1004, and seven years later he was elected to rule over the remaining tribes (2 Sam. 2.1-7 and 5.1-5). After the conquest of Jerusalem he made this Canaanite city his residence. In numerous campaigns David was able to subjugate all the neighbouring peoples, so that his kingdom also comprised a number of vassal states in addition to the heartland with its Israelite and Canaanite population. Even though David seems to have interfered little in the ancient rights of the once independent tribes, the changes necessary as a consequence of the establishment of the monarchy already began under his hegemony. The first cities were also founded during his reign from 1004 to 965, as could be demonstrated at Kinneret and on *Tell es-Seba'*. Under his son Solomon this urbanization and the accompanying transformation from a tribal society to the population of a state living in cities were taken further, although the consciousness of tribal identity remained at least to a certain extent. Great building programmes were carried out during the reign of Solomon

(965-926), and these have exerted a lasting influence on the cultural history.[12] The capital city was enlarged, with the addition of a palace and a temple, and throughout the whole country the new foundation or re-fortification of numerous cities took place, during which process the Canaanite population was totally integrated.

After the death of Solomon, the kingdom broke apart into the two states Israel and Judah. The reason for this break does not lie alone in the old opposition between north and south, which could only be kept under control by a powerful ruler who himself personified union, but also in the conflict between the demands of the state and the rights of the population, so that the break can finally be attributed to disputes about taxes and services (1 Kgs 12). The tribes which rebelled against the House of David remained loyal to the monarchical constitution, although rebellions brought about a frequent change of dynasty in Israel, while in Judah the dynasty of David was firmly established.

Under the monarchy, the urban way of life was also maintained until the end of both states. For the northern kingdom, Omri founded a new capital city at Samaria in 876, after several changes of residence. With the end of both states, the phenomenon of the Israelite city disappears. Israel was finally made into a province by the Assyrians in 722, after large portions of the former state territory had already been separated off from it in 733. After the conquest of Jerusalem by the Babylonians in 587 Judah suffered a similar fate to its identity as an individual state, accompanied by destruction and deportations. The history of settlement on nearly all the mounds which contain archaeological remains was curtailed by these two events, and where a new settlement followed, the continuity bears the signature of an Assyrian, Babylonian or Persian influence.

The state territory of the united kingdom comprised the region containing the settlements of the tribes and the last area under the authority of the Canaanite city-states. The consolidation of these two different territories was completed as an internal political event under Solomon by the division of Palestine into twelve administrative areas (1 Kgs 4.7-20), whereby Judah was excluded, for unknown reasons. Thus ancient Israel stretched 'from Dan to Beersheba' (Judg. 20.1; 1 Sam. 3.20, 2 Sam. 17.11). This ancient formula mentions the northern-most city of Dan, situated on a source of the Jordan, and the opposite

12. Cf. T. Ishida (ed.) *Studies in the Period of David and Solomon and other Essays* (1982); V. Fritz, 'Salomo', *MDOG* 117 (1985), pp. 47-67.

Figure 1. *Map of Palestine during the Iron Age*

outpost in the Negev. Although Beersheba was not the southernmost city, it constituted an urban focal point for the whole region. Within this area the Israelite settlements, until around 1000, were mostly situated in the mountains of Galilee, Ephraim and Judah, as well as in the high plateaux of the Transjordan, while the cities of the Canaanites mostly continued on in existence in the plains, such as that of Jesreel and the northern coastal area. Solomon had already handed over the plain of Acre to the Phoenicians of Tyre (1 Kgs 9.10-14). The southern coastal plain was the area inhabited by the Philistines with their five cities Ashkelon, Ashdod, Gat, Ekron and Gaza. Under the monarchy, a strong intermingling of the two population elements began, since the foundation of new cities took place without regard for older territorial boundaries. Thus numerous mounds of ruins dating from the Middle and Late Bronze Ages, such as at Hazor or Lachish, were newly occupied, and a widespread disappearance of old building traditions is evident in the former Canaanite cities. Thus, with urbanization, the various parts of the country were brought together to form one single state.

Although the form of the city in ancient Israel was an innovation of the period of the monarchy, there are only few references to it in the literary sources, since it was taken for granted as a natural cultural manifestation.[13] Where details are concerned, mention is made only of the gate, towers and city walls, whose function marks them as particular features. In its militant aspect, the city is radically different to the village. Temple and palace were to be found in the capital cities of Jerusalem and Samaria (1 Kgs 6 and 7). The references to a street of bakers in Jerusalem (Jer. 37.21) or a trading post of the Aramaeans of Damascus in Samaria (2 Kgs 7.1) point to the practice of crafts and trade in the capital cities, but nothing is mentioned about the layout and function of the cities. The nature and significance of the ancient Israelite cities can therefore only be inferred from archaeological examination.[14]

13. Cf. F.S. Frick, *The City in Ancient Israel* (1977); L. Rost, 'Die Stadt im Alten Testament', *ZDPV* 97 (1981), pp. 129-38.

14. Cf. on the archaeology H. Weippert, *Palästina in vorhellenistischer Zeit* (1988); K. Kenyon, *Royal Cities of the Old Testament* (1971); C. De Geus, 'The Profile of an Israelite City', *BA* 49 (1986), pp. 244-47.

Chapter 2

THE BEGINNINGS OF URBANIZATION

A process of urbanization took place twice in the region of the southern Levant: in Early Bronze Age II at the beginning of the third millennium, and in Middle Bronze Age II at the beginning of the second millennium. The two periods are separated from each other by an intervening period of several centuries, in which there were no cities but only small villages which were built predominantly in the peripheral areas.[1] The reasons for the interruption in urban culture are unknown, since this is a singular phenomenon which cannot be identified in other parts of the Near East. The first phase of the foundation of the cities in the third millennium is thus a separate period in itself, and did not have any direct influence on the renewed onset of urbanization in the second millennium.

City is the term applied to a form of communal living which is subject to particular preconditions, and which differs from other forms of human coexistence. Since conditions altered during the course of history, the criteria for a definition of the city in the period of the Early Bronze Age in the region of the southern Levant must be individually established. The formation of a vicious circle is to a certain extent unavoidable here, since such a determination can itself only be made on the basis of evidence from cities that have been excavated up to the present. However, while no city of the third millennium has been anywhere near

1. On this non-urban intermediate period see W.G. Dever, 'The "Middle Bronze I Period" in Syria and Palestine', in *Near Eastern Archaeology in the Twentieth Century: Essays in Honor of Nelson Glueck* (ed. A. Saunders; 1970), pp. 132-63; *idem*, 'The EB IV-MB I Horizon in Transjordan and Southern Palestine', *BASOR* 210 (1973), pp. 37-63; *idem*, 'New Vistas on the EB IV ("MB I") Horizon in Syria-Palestine', *BASOR* 237 (1980), pp. 65-84; E.D. Oren, 'The Early Bronze IV Period in Northern Palestine and its Cultural and Chronological Setting', *BASOR* 210 (1973), pp. 20-37; K. Prag, 'The Intermediate Early Bronze-Middle Bronze Age: An Interpretation of the Evidence from Transjordan, Syria and Lebanon', *Levant* 6 (1974), pp. 69-116; S. Richard, 'Toward a Consensus of Opinion on the End of the Early Bronze Age in Palestine-Transjordan', *BASOR* 237 (1980), pp. 5-34.

completely excavated, those parts of various sites that have been thus examined allow a clear definition to be made. The city is characterized by the following elements during the Early Bronze Age:

1. The city is of a certain size which differentiates it clearly from a village. The area which it covers is subject to large regional variations, but it never falls below a certain minimum. Of the cities founded in Early Bronze Age II, Megiddo covers an area of 6 hectares (*c.* 15 acres), Ai, Gezer and Arad around 10 hectares (*c.* 25 acres), while by contrast the city on *Tell esh-Sheikh 'Akhmed el-'Areinī* in the Shefela had an area of about 25 hectares (*c.* 62.5 acres).

2. The city is protected by a ring of walls, with access through gates or posterns. The type of fortification can be very varied and consists of a wall or rampart construction. A decisive factor is the creation of a system of defenses, constructed by the inhabitants to enable them to defend themselves from attacks or ambushes from outside.

3. Inside the city there are monumental buildings as well as residential houses; the former can cover a substantial part of the area enclosed by the wall. Among these are primarily the temple and the palace, which are often situated at the centre of the whole settlement or otherwise occupy a prominent position. Thus at the same time a social differentiation is indicated. Even though the form of rule cannot be more closely defined, the palace indicates the centralization of power in the person of the ruler.

4. The sum total of these elements eventually necessitated a certain degree of planning where the construction of the city was concerned. All of the houses had to be accessible from the city gate via streets. At the same time, the system of streets provided the drainage that became essential when it rained. The need for access obliged the inhabitants to position their houses so as to use the space available in the best possible way.

5. Communal life within the city presupposes a certain differentiation in society through the distribution of work. This is only visible in the architecture in exceptional cases, but it can be reckoned that in addition to farmers there were also craftsmen, traders and priests living in the city. The ruler thus occupied a position at the peak of the social order.

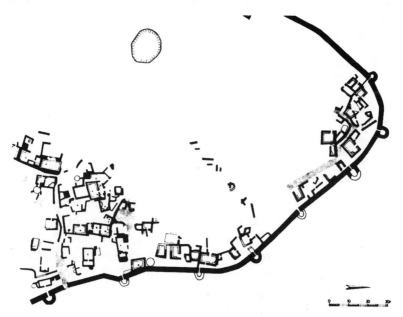

Figure 2. *Arad. City of the Early Bronze Age II.*

In numerous places, the building of permanent cities in Early Bronze Age II (2950–2650) is preceded by the open form of settlement of Early Bronze Age I.[2] This continuity in the history of settlement, as it can be seen in Megiddo, Beth-Shean, Ai, Jericho and Arad, indicates that the foundation of these cities is a local development, which was broadly independent of the changeover to an urban form of living in other parts of the Near East, since it had already partly taken place there during the second half of the fourth millennium.[3] Only a few cities such as Hazor

2.   See A. Kempinski, *The Rise of an Urban Culture. The Urbanisation of Palestine in the Early Bronze Age* (1978); R. Amiran, 'The Beginnings of Urbanisation in Canaan', in *Archaeology in the Twentieth Century*, pp. 83-100; P.W. Lapp, 'Palestine in the Early Bronze Age', in *Archaeology in the Twentieth Century*, pp. 101-31; S. Richard, 'The Early Bronze Age: The Rise and Collapse of Urbanism', *BA* 50 (1987), pp. 22-44.

3.   On urbanization in general cf. *City Invincible. A Symposium on Urbanization and Cultural Development in the Ancient Near East* (ed. C.H. Kraeling and R.M. Adams; 1960); *Courses Towards Urban Life. Archaeological Considerations of Some Cultural Alternatives* (ed. R.J. Braidwood and G.R. Willey; 1962); R.M. Adams, *The Evolution of Urban Society* (1966); *Man, Settlement and Urbanism* (ed. P. Ucko, R. Tringham and G.W. Dimbley; 1972); C.L. Redman,

and Beth-Shemesh were founded on hitherto unoccupied land at the beginning of Early Bronze Age II. Towards the end of this period a number of these cities were abandoned; however the foundation of another series of cities began in Early Bronze Age III (2650–2350). None of these cities survived the collapse which took place at the end of Early Bronze Age III.

As in the case of the settlements which preceded them, the new cities were mostly situated near wells in the plains or valleys, but they are occasionally found on slopes, such as at Kinneret, Ai or Arad. The city walls can vary considerably in width and differ from each other in the method of construction. In one case mudbrick walls from 2 to 6 m thick were built on stone foundations, with projecting semicircular or rectangular towers (cf. fig. 2). In another, the walls were brought to a width of 8 to 10 m or more through the fitting together of parallel segments and occasionally given particular protection through a *glacis* or ramp. The gate was independently secured by means of towers flanking it, without the development of a particular type of gate construction. Further points of access were offered by the numerous posterns in the wall, but these could also be under the control of a tower which afforded them particular protection.[4]

The dominant form in domestic architecture was the wide-room house, which had already been in use in the fourth millennium (fig. 2). Its floor was below ground level and it could be entered via two steps; benches ran along the walls, and a large flat stone served as a table. The basic form could be enlarged by the building of annexes and additional rooms, so that on occasion farmstead-like units were formed, surrounded by walls. Through subdivision or combination it was possible to create houses consisting of several rooms, in which the entrance came to be positioned in the shorter wall. The irregular way of building necessitated an irregular pattern of streets, which occasionally widened out to form small squares. The house form was also carried over into cultic architecture, such as is demonstrated by the wide-room temples in Megiddo, Ai and Jarmut.[5] The only palace has been found in Megiddo,

The Rise of Civilization, from the Early Farmers to Urban Society in the Ancient Near East (1978).

4. Cf. S.W. Helms, 'The Postern in the Early Bronze Age: Fortification of Palestine', *Levant* 10 (1975), pp. 133-50.

5. On temple construction see G.E. Wright, 'The Significance of Ai in the Third Millenium BC', in *Archäologie und Altes Testament. Festschrift für K. Galling*

in Strata XVII and XVI, situated in a boundaried precinct in the south east of the city and can be dated to Early Bronze Age III (fig. 3). The parts that have been excavated allow for the identification of a sensibly planned building on a strict, right-angled alignment, with integrated courts and long corridors, which allowed independent access to all rooms. In comparison to the simple house forms, the palace exhibits a definite further stage of development, which might possibly be due to foreign influences.[6]

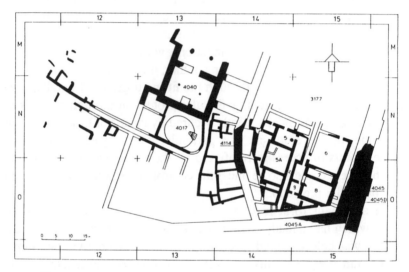

Figure 3. *Megiddo. Palace of the Early Bronze Age III (Stratum XVI).*

Of a completely singular nature is a building in *Khirbet el-Kerak*, which can be designated a large granary on the grounds of parallels in Egypt and in the Aegean.[7] It consists of a large substructure of quarried stone,

(1970), pp. 299-319; I. Dunayevsky and A. Kempinski, 'The Megiddo Temples', *ZDPV* 89 (1973), pp. 161-187; H. Weippert, *Palästina in vorhellenistischer Zeit* (1988), p. 163, Abb. 3.11.

6.   A typological characterization of the palace in Megiddo is made very difficult because of the incomplete nature of its ground plan; however certain points of correspondence with the palace in Sector P on *Tell Inghārra*, dating from the third millennium, cannot be ignored. Cf. E. Heinrich, *Die Paläste im alten Mesopotamien* (1984), pp. 23ff. with Fig. 14. At present, however, the layout of this palace is puzzling.

7.   The building with corn silos in *Khirbet el-Kerak* has parallels in Egypt as well as in the Aegean and was developed from a building form that had been taken over, cf. O. Höckmann, 'Zu dem kykladischen Gebäudemodell von Melos',

measuring 40 × 30 m in size, in which there are nine circular recesses which are to be defined as round silos with dome-like covers (fig. 4).

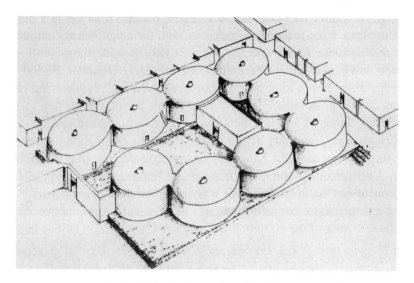

Figure 4. *Khirbet-el-Kerak. Granaries of the Early Bronze Age III.*

The whole complex is accessible from the east, where a 25 m long corridor leads into a court which is bordered in the west by a wide-room house.

In its entirety, the urbanization which took place during Early Bronze II and III constitutes a simple stage of development. Only the rudiments of an orderly method of building are visible. The layout of the city does not exhibit planning of any kind, and the differentiation that might have existed in society is hardly documented by the architecture. Domestic architecture with its central element, the wide-room house, has undergone little in the way of development, and large buildings are only found sporadically. Due to their immensity, the fortifications are extremely effective, but the gates are simple openings in the wall, protected by towers. Taken as a whole, however, the systems of defences exhibit a high standard. A central rule can be discerned from the palace at Megiddo, and by the same token the building with a total of nine grain silos in *Khirbet el-Kerak* points to the practice of a storage-based economy, with the possible prerequisite of a central administration.

Istanbuler Mitteilungen 25 (1975), pp. 269-99; J.D. Currid, 'The Beehive Granaries of Ancient Palestine', *ZDPV* 101 (1985), pp. 97-109.

In spite of their predominantly agrarian character, the Early Bronze
Age cities did not simply exist in isolation. Although agriculture clearly
formed the economic foundation of the cities, weapons and tools of
copper must have had their origin in trade, inasmuch as various other
finds indicate wide-reaching connections with the neighbouring cultures.
Various ceramic forms and the use of cylinder and stamp seals on
vessels have parallels in the cultures of the Early Dynastic Period in
Mesopotamia; thus a long-lasting contact with the land between the two
rivers can be postulated.[8] Trade contacts with Egypt are attested to by
numerous imported articles, the name of Narmer in incised graffiti, and
seal impressions; military action by the Pharaohs or an Egyptian overlordship during the Old Kingdom cannot however be deduced from
them.[9] Furthermore, the numerous vessels imported into Egypt allow
the conclusion that intensive trade was carried on during that period.[10]

As a whole, these contacts seem only to have had a minimal influence
on the character of the culture. The Early Bronze Age foundations in the
southern Levant are a far cry from the size and standards of the
Mesopotamian cities of the fourth and third millennia, such as they are
encountered at *Habuba Kabira'* or Uruk.[11] Neither, apparently, was
there any adoption or development of a system of writing, since until
now no evidence of this has been discovered. Thus a system of writing is
not a necessary precondition for the organization of a city, as long as the

8.   J.B. Hennesy, *The Foreign Relations of Palestine during the Early Bronze
Age* (1967); cf. A. Ben-Tor, *Cylinder Seals of Third Millenium Palestine* (*BASOR*
Supplement 22; 1978); P. Beck, 'The Cylinder Seal Impressions from Beth
Ha'Emeq', *Tel Aviv* 3 (1976), pp. 120-26.

9.   S. Yeivin, 'Early Contacts Between Canaan and Egypt', *IEJ* 10 (1960),
pp. 193-203; S. Yeivin, 'Further Evidence of Narmer at 'Gat', *Oriens Antiquus* 2
(1963), pp. 205-13; 'Additional Notes on the Early Relations between Canaan and
Egypt', *JNES* 27 (1968), pp. 37-50; R. Amiran, 'The Egyptian Alabaster Vessels
from Ai', *IEJ* 20 (1970), pp. 170-79; 'An Egyptian Jar Fragment with the Name of
Narmer', *IEJ* 24 (1974), pp. 4-12; R. Gophna, 'Egyptian Immigration into Southern
Canaan during the First Dynasty?', *Tel Aviv* 3 (1976), pp. 31-37; A.R. Schulman,
'The Egyptian Seal Impressions from 'En Besor', *'Atiqot* ES 11 (1976), pp. 16-26;
A.R. Schulman, 'More Egyptian Seal Impressions from 'En Besor', *'Atiqot* ES 14
(1980), pp. 17-33; A. Ben-Tor, 'The Relations between Egypt and the Land of
Canaan during the Third Millenium BC', *AJA* 85 (1981), pp. 449-52.

10. Cf. the survey in W. Helck, *Die Beziehungen Ägyptens zu Vorderasien im
3. und 2. Jahrtausend v. Chr.* (2nd edn, 1971), pp. 25-37.

11. Cf. the summary in E. Heinrich, 'Architektur von der früh- bis zur
neusumerischen Zeit', in W. Orthmann, *Der alte Orient* (1975), pp. 131-58.

latter remains strongly agricultural in nature and does not exceed a certain size. After a development of only 600 years, this urban culture disappeared completely around 2350, for unknown reasons, while it continued in Syria.[12]

12. The history of the settlement at Ebla can serve as an example. Cf. P. Matthiae, *Ebla, An Empire Rediscovered* (1981), pp. 65-111.

Chapter 3

THE CANAANITE CITY

The new beginning of urbanization at the start of the second millennium represents a new culture, which exhibits no connection of any kind with that of Early Bronze Ages II und III.[1] As this culture appears to have possessed a full character of its own when the first cities were founded along the coast at the beginning of Middle Bronze Age II A, it cannot have developed in Palestine itself, but was brought in by new immigrants. The origin of these people is unknown, but various elements in their material culture demonstrate a connection with the Syrian and Mesopotamian area.[2] In accordance with Egyptian and Biblical linguistic usage the people can be referred to as Canaanites who, according to their names, were Semites.

The cities, some of which were extremely large, were mainly built in two 'waves', during the twentieth and eighteenth centuries. Here, Early Bronze Age hill settlements were sometimes refortified—as at Dan, Hazor, Megiddo, Shechem, Afek, Gezer and Jericho—but occasionally settlements were established on land which had hitherto not been built on, such as at Acre, Beth-El or Beth-Shemesh. In a few cases

---

1. On the history of the period cf. B. Mazar, 'The Middle Bronze Age in Canaan', *IEJ* 18 (1968), pp. 65-97 = *The Early Biblical Period. Historical Studies* (1986), 1-33; W.G. Dever, 'The Middle Bronze Age. The Zenith of the Urban Canaanite Era', *BA* 50 (1987), pp. 149-77; M. Broshi and R. Gophna, 'Middle Bronze II Palestine. Its Settlement and Population', *BASOR* 261 (1986), pp. 73-90; A. Kempinski, *Syrien und Palästina (Kanaan) in der letzten Phase der Mittelbronze II B-Zeit (1650–1570 v. Chr.)* (1983).

2. Cf. J. Kaplan, 'Mesopotamian Elements in the Middle Bronze Age II Culture of Palestine', *JNES* 30 (1971), pp. 293-307; G.R.H. Wright, *Ancient Building in South Syria and Palestine* (1985), pp. 43-59. By contrast, the view that there were local developments in the country is also represented, cf. J.N. Tubb, 'The MB II: A Period in Palestina: Its Relationship with Syria and its Origin', *Levant* 15 (1983), pp. 49-62.

an unfortified settlement preceded the fortified city, as could be demonstrated at Shechem or at Gezer. The cities exhibit clear differences in their size: Jericho covered 3 hectares (*c.* 7.5 acres), but even Achzib on the coast and Lachish were relatively small, covering 7 hectares (*c.* 17.5 acres). Megiddo extended over 10 hectares, while Dan and Acre reached an average size with their 20 hectares (*c.* 50 acres). The large cities, for example Ashkelon or the city of *el-Kabrī*, covered around 60 hectares (*c.* 150 acres), while Hazor at 80 hectares was the largest city in the country. There were numerous villages in the immediate vicinity of the cities, and they were probably under the rule of the respective city-state.[3] In addition, the individual rulers also constructed forts, manned by troops, to maintain security in the area of their influence.

From the time of the twelfth Dynasty (1991–1785) in Egypt onwards, the Pharaohs claimed authority over Canaan, even if such a claim could not be constantly upheld at all times.[4] The end of Middle Bronze Age II B around 1550 constitutes a break, inasmuch as several of the cities which had been destroyed, such as Dan, *el-Kabrī*, Gibeon and Jericho were not rebuilt. The Egyptian overlordship was established once again by the Pharaohs of the eighteenth Dynasty (1540–1295). During the course of the Late Bronze Age (1550–1200), a certain decline in the urban culture is to be noted, and this continued on into Iron Age I (1200–1000).[5] At numerous locations, the area built upon was reduced in size and the fortifications were not brought back into use on the former scale. The reasons for this cannot be discerned; it can, however, be surmised that they stem from a military and economic situation of little stability, as is reflected in the letters of the city rulers to the Pharaoh from the time of Amenophis III and IV. Numerous cities such as Dan or Gibeon were not the only ones to have been abandoned at the end of the Middle Bronze Age; others such as Gezer and Ashdod were severely

---

3.   For the area of the coastal plain see R. Gophna and P. Beck, 'The Rural Aspects of the Settlement Patterns of the Coastal Plain in the Middle Bronze Age II', *Tel Aviv* 8 (1981), pp. 45-80.

4.   Cf. W. Helck, *Die Beziehungen Ägyptens zu Vorderasien während des 3. und 2. Jahrtausend v. Chr.* (2nd edn, 1971); J.M. Weinstein, 'Egyptian Relations with Palestine in the Middle Kingdom', *BASOR* 217 (1975), pp. 1-16.

5.   Cf. J.M. Weinstein, 'The Egyptian Empire in Palestine: A Reassessment', *BASOR* 241 (1981), pp. 1-28; R. Gonen, 'Urban Canaan in the Late Bronze Age Period', *BASOR* 253 (1984), pp. 61-73; S. Ahituv, 'Economic Factors in the Egyptian Conquest of Canaan', *IEJ* 28 (1978), pp. 93-105.

reduced in size and there is also a certain debilitation noticeable within the individual cities themselves.

Megiddo

As Megiddo is the only city in Palestine of which areas containing all levels of the Middle and Late Bronze Age have been excavated, it offers the possibility of a comparative study of successive occupation levels.[6]

In Stratum XIII the city was refounded and fortified at the beginning of Middle Bronze Age II A, so that the cultic precinct that had been created in the vicinity of temple 4040 during Stratum XIV A was retained and surrounded by a wall. In contrast to this occupation level, the city in stratum XII was completely replanned. A small building was constructed in the cultic precinct, and surrounded by stelae; this constitutes the first step to a new type of cultic building.[7] To the west of the cultic precinct there was a large palace, of which however only parts of a tract of rooms have been excavated; these are arranged around one or more courts. Between the *temenos* and the palace there were more administrative buildings. To the east and south of the *temenos* there were private houses of the courtyard-house type. In the area of the city wall, these houses abut onto it. The entrance to the city was via a gate on the north side.

The city exhibits a planned layout. The situation of the cultic precinct was dictated by tradition, and the position of the palace could be due to a desired proximity to the sacred place. These two important areas in the eastern part of the city were easily reached from the gate. There is a certain regularity behind the positioning of the private houses, with lines of streets of about 2 m in width running through them; here, the high degree of right-angled alignment points to prior planning and determination of the limits of the area available for building.

This city-planning was mostly retained during the many reconstruction phases in the course of the second millennium, but individual sectors

6.   The reconstruction of the individual settlement levels follows I. Dunayevski and A. Kempinski, 'The Megiddo Temples', *ZDPV* 89 (1973), pp. 161-87 and A. Kempinski, *Megiddo. A City State and Royal Center in North Israel* (1989).

7.   The assumption made by C. Epstein that Temple 2048 was built as early as Stratum XII, in 'An Interpretation of the Megiddo Sacred Area during Middle Bronze II', *IEJ* 15 (1965), pp. 204-19, fails to stand up to a closer examination of the stratification.

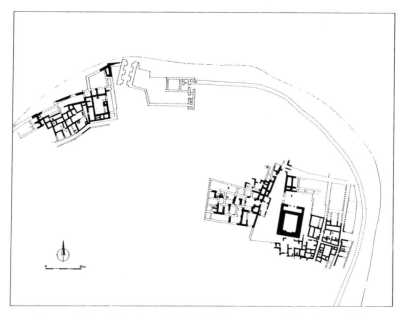

Figure 5. *Megiddo. City of the Middle Bronze Age II B (Stratum X).*

were sometimes given a completely new form and thus greatly altered, as can be seen from the city in Stratum X during Middle Bronze Age II B (fig. 5). A temple in the form of a long house with an entrance hall was built within the cultic precinct. The *temenos* wall was abandoned, and delimitation of the precinct effected through the positioning of outbuildings in the north and east, so that an open area was retained in front of the temple. The palace was completely rebuilt on the site of the old one. Although the bad state of preservation does not permit recognition of the principles behind its construction, it does however differ radically in the form of its layout from its predecessor, since an arrangement of the rooms around courts is no longer discernible. The temple and the palace are separated from one another by an open square, which tapers to a point in a northerly direction. The newly-constructed private houses to the west of the temple precinct were set together to form *insulae*, with streets running between them. No *insula* has been completely excavated, but the division into residential blocks, each with several houses next to each other, is clearly visible. Even though the city gate in this occupation level has not been uncovered, its position on the north side of the city can be presumed, since the ascending path on this side was used for centuries, down into the Iron

Age. The city wall was not rebuilt, but the houses which have been excavated on the northern boundary formed a closed ring for the defence of the city.

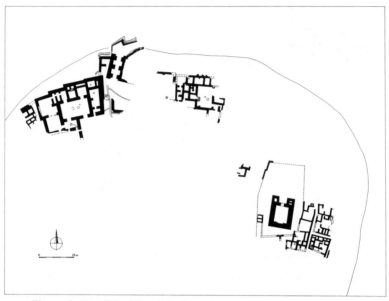

Figure 6. *Megiddo. City of the Late Bronze Age II A (Stratum VIII).*

In spite of the retention of individual elements, the Late Bronze Age city of Stratum VIII exhibits several significant alterations (fig. 6). Only the temple remained on its old site, but here, instead of the entrance hall, two towers were constructed which flanked the entrance. The temple precinct was independently separated from the residential areas by means of a new wall. To the east of the temple there were further private houses of the courtyard-house type, while the palace in the west was apparently not rebuilt. Two new palaces were built in the north of the city, however, but they have not been completely excavated. Of these, palace 2041 was situated south west of the city gate, while the other palace 5020 was to the east of the gate. Both exhibit the grouping of the rooms around open courts that is typical of the period. Their proximity can possibly be explained by the fact that, during Late Bronze Age II, Megiddo was under Egyptian hegemony and functioned as a provincial capital, so that here a high-ranking Egyptian administrator resided alongside the local ruler. The repositioning of the palace near the gate could be due to the need for better access. The construction of the gate corresponds to a common type with three pairs of pilasters at each of the two towers. The existence of a city wall has not been demonstrated, but to the west of the gate the external walls of palace 2041 with their projecting sections constitute an adequately strong fortification.

Leaving aside the various changes that are apparent when a comparison is made with Stratum X, the city in Stratum VIII exhibits the same principles of layout. The temple is in the centre of a cultic precinct, which is separated from the rest of the city. The palaces are extremely extensive in size and in terms of area take in a large part of the city territory; they are conveniently placed where communications and commerce were concerned, but do not constitute the centre of the city area. The house units are bordered by networks of streets, which run straight for long distances and cross each other at right angles.

The city lasted in this form into Stratum VII A (fig. 7), which was destroyed around 1150. Here, however, certain indications of decline are not to be overlooked; the temple was of a less monumental construction, palace 5020 had disappeared, and palace 2041 had been reduced in size. The building which took place in the southern part was extremely irregular in nature and does not allow the identification of a clear pattern of streets. (There are, however, no criteria for comparison in this quarter of the city, since its older occupation layers have not been excavated). On the whole, the plan in general corresponds to that of the previous city.

The layout and construction of the city are of the same standard in the occupation layers of Strata XII to VII A, which points both to great competence in the planning as well as a decisiveness in the execution of the plans. The recession in urban culture in the second half of the twelfth century after the end of Stratum VII A is especially apparent at Megiddo. There were only minimal alterations to the layout in the city in Strata X to VII A (figs. 5–7). By contrast, the settlement of Stratum VI A, which is still to be defined as Canaanite,[8] has a completely different concept behind it (fig. 8). The temple and the palace have disappeared, and the gate has shrunk to two small chambers flanking the passageway through it. There are larger buildings on both sides of the gate, but the remainder of the city area exhibits an irregular pattern of domestic building, which does not allow recognition of any kind of planning. Even though complete ground plans of houses have not been preserved, the establishment of a comprehensive pattern of streets and adjacent

8.   The transition to the Israelite city is first indicated at Megiddo in Stratum V A, contra Y. Aharoni, 'New Aspects of the Israelite Occupation in the North', in *Near Eastern Archaeology in the Twentieth Century* (1970), pp. 254-67.

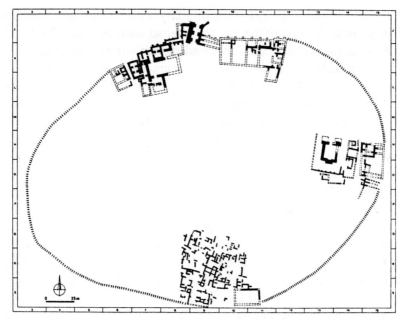

Figure 7. *Megiddo. City of the Late Bronze Age II B/Iron Age I (Stratum VII A).*

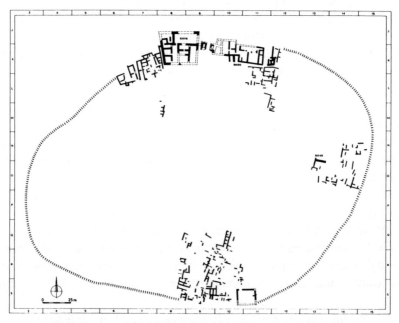

Figure 8. *Megiddo. Settlement of the Iron Age I (Stratum VI A).*

residential blocks is no longer recognizable. The houses were constructed according to the immediate needs of the inhabitants, without any principle of order or planning. The breakdown of political order is reflected in the abandonment of planned construction in individual parts of the city.

Individual Elements

All the cities of the Middle Bronze Age exhibit the high level of urbanization which, with certain detractions, continued during the Late Bronze Age. Apart from the city wall, all elements differ from those found in the Early Bronze Age cities, but they can already be recognized as early as the close of the third millennium in Syria. Since the Syrian cities existed in unbroken continuity, it can be reckoned that numerous building forms and techniques were assimilated from this area via the new settlers, or were brought in and then developed further inside Palestine. In the different locations, the various elements present a good picture of Canaanite city culture as it existed in the second millenium down to around 1200 BC.

In the case of fortifications, an enormous expansion can be discerned.[9] Four different systems of city walls can be defined (fig. 9); the method of construction of three of them is far ahead of that practised in the Early Bronze Age:

1. *The Wall with Glacis (Ramp)*
The city wall, 2.5–4.0 m thick, was further secured by a sloping ramp on the outside. This simple wall could be built of stones, as at Megiddo, Shechem and Afek, or of mud brick on a stone foundation, as at Gezer. In both cases, the wall was reinforced by rectangular towers.

2. *The Earth Rampart*
This form of rampart consists of an enormous amount of deposited material, which at Acre, for example, exhibits a height of 20 m and a width of 60 m at the base. Attempts were made there to increase its stability through alteration in the direction in which the material was deposited and the use of different materials.

9.   Cf. P.J. Parr, 'The Origin of the Rampart Fortifications of Middle Bronze Age Palestine and Syria', *ZDPV* 84 (1968), pp. 18-45; J. Kaplan, 'Further Aspects of The Middle Bronze Age II Fortifications in Palestine', *ZDPV* 91 (1975), pp. 1-17.

3. *The Earth Rampart with Wall and Glacis (Ramp)*

Occasionally the combination of rampart and city wall is such that the wall is situated on a bank of material which has been deposited in order to raise the area, whereby the external slope could still be particularly secured by means of a glacis and ditch.

4. *The Earth Rampart with a Wall at its Centre*

A ramp was thrown up on either side of a wall which measured up to 6 m in width, so that the wall was covered by the deposited material to a certain height. The city wall then projected above both ramps and thus acquired its greatest strength as a fortification device. Use of this type of rampart could be ascertained at Dan and Hazor through sections.

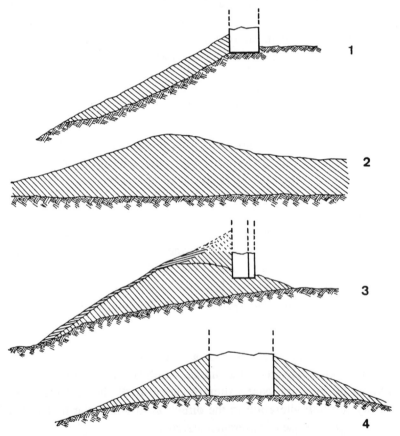

Figure 9. *Schematic section through different types of defenses of the Middle Bronze Age II: 1 Wall with glacis. 2. Earth rampart. 3. Earth rampart with wall and glacis. 4. Earth rampart with wall as core.*

All of these types of construction were employed from the beginning of
Middle Bronze Age II A onwards, with the earthen rampart constituting
a completely new device that ensured both the necessary protection
from erosion and at the same time increased the possibility of defence.
Parallel to the reinforcement of the city fortifications the gate structure
was developed as an independent building.[10] Apart from a few singular
solutions with right-angled twisting access there are three different types
of gate to be discerned (fig. 10). These were in use simultaneously in different places, so that the question of their chronological development has
to remain open, even though the three forms exhibit a close relationship
to one another:

1. *The Gate between Two Towers*
The entrance passage runs between two solid towers, which were placed
in a way that they projected both outside and inside the walls. Sections
of the towers projected into the entrance passage in the form of three
pairs of short walls, the so-called pilasters, which made the way through
the gate additionally narrow and served to protect the doors themselves.
The best example of solid gate towers was discovered at Gezer.

2. *The Gate between Two Towers with Adjacent Rooms*
This type differs from that of the solid gate construction in that in both
of the gate towers there were rooms, which were at least partly accessible
from the entrance passage through the gate, and were used by those
guarding the gate. Sometimes the upper part of the gate construction
and the crest of the wall could be reached directly via a stairway. In some
cases the rooms in the gate towers were only accessible from above;
thus they can only have served as storerooms. The pilasters could extend
so far forward that small rooms were created between them. Gates of
this kind were widely distributed during Middle Bronze Age II B.

3. *The Chambered Gate*
In this type of gate construction, the pilasters on both sides of the passage extended to such a degree that rooms of medium size were formed.
The pilasters were incorporated into a wall at an oblique angle to the city
wall, so that the towers were done away with; thus the gate construction

---

10. Z. Herzog, *Das Stadttor in Israel und in den Nachbarländern* (1986), pp. 37-
75; B. Gregori, '"Three-Entrance" City-Gates of the Middle Bronze Age in Syria and
Palestine', *Levant* 18 (1986), pp. 83-102.

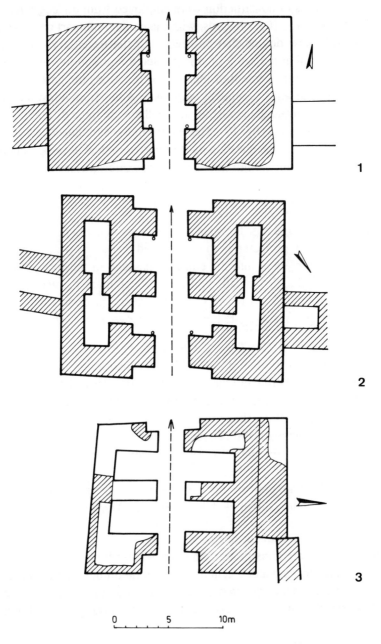

Figure 10. *Gates of the Middle Bronze Age II: 1. The gate between two towers (Gezer). 2. The gate between two towers wtih rooms and chambers (Hazor). 3. The camber-gate (Dan).*

with its four rooms—the chambers—acquired a building-like character. This type is relatively rare; the best example is the completely preserved gate of Middle Bronze Age II A at Dan.[11] Where there are only two pairs of pilasters the number of the chambers is reduced from four to two. The development of the chambered gate seems to have been brought about through the placing of ramparts, which rendered the construction of towers pointless.

Thus there are a number of solutions for the construction of the gate which were still unknown during the Early Bronze Age. An independent building has developed out of the passageway through the wall secured by towers. This not only makes possible an excellent defence of the access into the city, but in peacetime it also allows for the control of traffic passing through. For such a purpose, the size of the cities necessitated the construction of several gates, which could be built in completely different ways. Thus in both Shechem and Hazor two gates were brought to light, although the existence of more gates can be assumed in the case of Hazor. Only after the idea of a gate had been conceived could the purpose served by the extraordinary reinforcement of the system of defences be fulfilled.

The building works in the city exhibit a decisive change in the form of the new type of domestic house. Predominant now is the courtyard house with its several variations. The characteristic feature of the courtyard house is the arrangement of rooms around a court, in which the court is bordered on one, two, three, or all four sides by rooms of different sizes (cf. figs. 4–6). Here, an almost rectangular ground plan for the whole house was often achieved. The entrance led into the court, which provided access to the rooms as well as light and air, since as a rule the rooms were either windowless or had only very small windows. It was only when the court was completely enclosed by rooms that the visitor first entered a vestibule. The house could achieve a considerable size through the addition of further tracts of rooms;[12] thus there are significant differences apparent between the various units.

In the case of the courtyard houses, there are numerous variations of the ground plan and layout, without it being possible to discern the function of the rooms in detail. The simplest form is the arrangement of rooms

11. A. Biran, 'The Triple Arched Gate of Laish at Tel Dan', *IEJ* 34 (1984), pp. 1-19.

12. Cf. A. Kempinski, *Syrien und Palästina (Kanaan) in der letzten Phase der Mittelbronze II B-Zeit (1650–1550 v. Chr.)* (1983), pp. 174-78.

in a row on one of the long sides of the courtyard. When there are rooms on two sides of the courtyard these can be either opposite each other or in a way joining in one corner. The layout of more rooms along the sides of the courtyard often leads to a reduction in the size of the courtyard. As the *insula* at Megiddo Stratum XII indicates, the different variants could be found alongside each other in rows (cf. fig. 4). The courtyard type of house developed during the third millennium in Mesopotamia and had since become widely distributed in all forms.[13] It is probable that there is a cultural and historical connection here, in that the new settlers brought this type of building with them from there, or acquired it through intermediate stages. Both the subdivision of the courtyard through stone pillars and the creation of semi-open rooms are occasionally observed.

None of the numerous palaces of this period have been completely excavated; thus all assertions are subject to the limitations imposed by the incomplete nature of the plans available. The term 'palace' signifies a building which in its dimensions far exceeds those of the normal private house and thus is to be taken as the residence of the ruler. Palatial architecture in the country was subject to great changes. Not one of the Middle Bronze Age palaces lasted on into the Late Bronze Age.[14] A common feature of all the palaces is the large central courtyard, around which the rooms are arranged. In individual cases two courtyards were set out next to each other. Due to the bad state of preservation, the underlying concept with its divisions into reception, living and commercial areas is not recognizable. The exceptional regularity of the layout is characteristic; this is visible in the palace at Megiddo Stratum XII, or the palace in the lower city of Hazor (cf. fig. 4), but the actual features exhibit great differences of detail. The presence of the palaces confirms the existence of a city-state, controlled by a local ruler, at Hazor, Shechem, Megiddo, Afek and Lachish. Originally this type of palace was based on the form of the courtyard house, but it represents an independent development in the building tradition, which probably took place outside the country.[15]

13. Cf. E. Heinrich, 'Haus', *RLA* IV (1973), pp. 176-220, particularly 208ff.

14. Cf. V. Fritz, 'Paläste während der Bronze- und Eisenzeit in Palästina', *ZDPV* 99 (1983), pp. 1-42. For the Middle Bronze Age palace at Lachish see D. Ussishkin, 'Excavations at Tel Lachish 1978–1983; Second Preliminary Report', *Tel Aviv* 10 (1983), pp. 97-175, particularly pp. 104-108.

15. In view of the fact that an examination of domestic and palace architecture in Syria has yet to be made, the possible connections as far as Mesopotamia cannot yet

In the Late Bronze Age, the closed aspect of the palace complex was abandoned in favour of a more marked division into individual units, such as is particularly noticeable in the palaces to the west of the gate at Megiddo deriving Strata VIII to VII A (cf. fig. 6). The individual sections are clearly divided off from each other, but are again arranged around inner courts, so that a certain continuity in building tradition can be discerned. A definition of the function of the different parts is not possible; however, the arrangement of the groups of rooms makes it probable that the tracts of rooms serving various functions were separated from one another.

With the long-room temple, a completely new building form in cultic architecture prevailed over the Early Bronze Age broad-room temple, although the latter still remained in use. The new type was widely distributed in the form of an ante-temple in Syria during the second millennium, and was taken over from there, but is ultimately based on the *megaron* house form, the existence of which has already been proved in Anatolia in the third millennium.[16] With the adoption of the form, the original prototype was altered in that, instead of the open vestibule, at Megiddo and Shechem two towers were constructed in front of the building, flanking the entrance. At Shechem, an altar was found a certain distance in front of the entrance, and a similar altar is likewise to be expected at Megiddo. Simple long-room temples were situated in Hazor as well as at *Tell Abū Hawām* and *Tell Mubārak*.

Other further forms of monumental cultic architecture existed beside this predominant type. The temple in Sector H at Hazor still had a broad inner room, but had been changed into a long house through towers set in front of it. The Late Bronze Age temples of Beth-Shean and Lachish have an almost rectangular main room and a room at a raised level, accessible via a stairway, which housed the image of the god. The origin of this type has not yet been established; it probably reflects an Egyptian influence.[17] Other smaller sanctuaries do not follow any recognizable building tradition and are probably the result of local developments.

be ascertained. See E. Heinrich, *Die Paläste im alten Mesopotamien* (1984).

16. Cf. M. Ottoson, *Temples and Cult Places in Palestine* (1980); G.R.H. Wright, 'Pre-Israelite Temples in the Land of Canaan', *PEQ* 103 (1971), pp. 17-32; V. Fritz, 'Der Tempel Salomos im Licht der neueren Forschung', *MDOG* 112 (1980), pp. 53-68.

17. Chr. Clamer and D. Ussishkin, 'A Canaanite Temple at Tell Lachish', *BA* 40 (1977), pp. 71-76; cf. the discussion in H. Weippert, *Palästina in vorhellenistischer Zeit* (1988), pp. 284-90.

History

Details about the history of the cities are only known in a few cases, since the sources are extremely sporadic in nature. To date, archives have not been discovered in Palestine, but the twelve clay tablets from Taanach, which contain letters and lists dating from the fifteenth century, show that documentation appropriate to the exigencies of the times must have existed in Palestine. The following sources for the history of the cities have been preserved in Egypt:

> Execration texts[18]
> The topographical lists[19]
> The Pharaohs' campaign reports[20]
> Letters in cuneiform from Amarna[21]

While the texts relating to execration and the lists of cities only mention place names, the campaign reports offer concrete information about the conquests of the Pharaohs, and the so-called Amarna Letters provide an insight into the relations of the city-states with one another. Thus historical knowledge is restricted to a number of momentary glimpses, as can be shown in the case of Megiddo.

Megiddo is not mentioned in the execration texts. This observation does not however permit any further inferences, since this group of texts does not represent a systematic listing of all the cities in Canaan. The oldest record comes from the so-called annals of Tuthmosis III (1479–1425), in which Megiddo is mentioned together with Kadesh on the Orontes as a member of an anti-Egyptian coalition.[22] The battle against the Egyptians under Tuthmosis III at Megiddo in 1468 ended with the

18. K. Sethe, *Ächtung feindlicher Fürsten, Völker und Dinge auf altägyptischen Tongefäßscherben des Mittleren Reiches* (1926); G. Posener, *Princes et Pays d'Asie et de Nubie* (1940).

19. Compiled by J. Simons, *Handbook for the Study of Egyptian Topographical Lists Relating to Western Asia* (1937).

20. Translated by J.H. Breasted, *Ancient Records of Egypt* (5 vols.; repr., 1926 [1906]).

21. J.A. Knudtzon, *Die El-Amarna-Tafeln* (repr., 1964 [1915]); A.F. Rainey, *El Amarna Tablets 359–79* (1978). The letters are referred to by the abbreviation EA with the appropriate number.

22. Translated by E. Edel, in K. Galling, *Textbuch zur Geschichte Israels* (3rd edn, 1979), pp. 14-20. See in addition A. Alt, 'Pharao Thutmosis III in Palästina', *PJ* 10 (1914), pp. 53-99.

defeat of the Canaanite rulers and the institution of Egyptian overlord-ship in Canaan. Megiddo was besieged by the Egyptian army in connex-ion with the campaign and only surrendered after seven months' siege.[23] Even if the latter is only to be taken as a round figure, the length of the period of resistance bears witness to the strength of the city. Megiddo was also mentioned in the Palestine lists of Tuthmosis III, in accordance with its significance.

There was probably an Egyptian garrison stationed in Megiddo; thus the city served as a base for operations in the time of Amenophis II (1427–1401).[24] This is referred to by letter 5 from Taanach, in which the ruler there is ordered to send men to Megiddo.[25] In a papyrus, which can likewise be dated to the time of Amenophis II, Megiddo is men-tioned among the cities of Canaan whose representatives at Pharaoh's court were supplied with corn and beer.[26] Several letters from Prince Biridiya of Megiddo to the Pharaoh were found in the archive at Amarna (EA 242-246.265). These are evidence for a certain responsibil-ity of the local ruler for enforced agricultural labour in the whole region. The threat posed by Lab'aya, the power-hungry ruler of Shechem, who also appears to be a troublemaker in other respects, ends with his murder. The reading of one final reference in a list of Seti I is not abso-lutely certain. The close connection with Egypt from the fifteenth to the twelfth century is also documented through numerous Egyptian finds from the occupation layers which have been excavated. Here the final mention of names in the form of cartouches of Ramses III and Ramses VI marks the end of Egyptian hegemony.

These references only provide little detail about the long period of time covered by Canaanite culture. Inscriptions on buildings, lists of kings, or biographies are missing to date, as are commercial texts. It must be reckoned here that a community of this size could not exist without written documentation of purchases, contracts and legal judg-ments, especially since a fragment of the Epic of Gilgamesh on a clay

23. The text is on a granite stele in the Temple of Amon at Napata in Nubia. Translated by E. Edel, in Galling, *Textbuch zur Geschichte Israels*, pp. 20f. See also A. Alt, 'Zu Thutmosis' III Kampf um Megiddo', *PJ* 32 (1936), pp. 10-18.

24. Cf. Aharoni, *The Land of the Bible*, pp. 166-69.

25. W.F. Albright, 'A Prince of Taanach in the 15th Cent. BC', *BASOR* 94 (1944), pp. 12-27; A. Malamat, 'Campaigns of Amenhotep II and Thutmose IV to Canaan', in *Studies in the Bible* (Scripta Hierosolymitana 8; 1961), pp. 218-31.

26. Cf. C. Epstein, 'A New Appraisal of Some Lines from a Long-Known Papyrus', *JEA* 49 (1953), pp. 49-56.

tablet and an inscribed clay model of a liver, as well as the letters which have been preserved, indicate a connection with cuneiform literature.[27] Thus the actual history of the city is a mystery. More is known only about a few events during the campaign of Thutmosis III in 1468 and the rule of Biridiya around 1370. Nevertheless, the sources confirm the powerful position of the city, and this is also documented in the remains of the individual occupation levels.

Decline

In contrast to the beginnings of urbanization in the third millennium, the city in the second millennium is fully developed in all aspects. Its layout exhibits a complex structure, in which the various necessities and precepts for the life of a structured community find their expression. Readiness to defend itself, domestic culture, the practice of cult, and a claim to supremacy are all manifested in the picture presented of a city that has been constituted according to certain principles of order. The city could only exist when it exerted simultaneous supremacy over the surrounding countryside worked by its inhabitants. The city-state thus included a number of smaller settlements. Next to agriculture there was the work of the craftsman who made products for daily use, such as the pottery and the weapons and tools of bronze which have been found in great quantity.

In all aspects, the Canaanite city represents a high form of culture. The volume of imported ceramics attests an intensive keen trade with Cyprus and the Aegean.[28] Especially during Late Bronze Age II B, an almost unlimited autonomy of the Canaanite cities is to be assumed in spite of the nominal overlordship of Egypt, although the Pharaohs kept their own bases in Gaza and Beth-Shean. However, the culture already exhibits a certain decline during the course of the Late Bronze Age. The size of the cities was reduced and their strength which was manifested in the fortifications diminished. This development does not however explain

27. A. Goetze and S. Levy, 'Fragment of the Gilgamesh Epic from Megiddo', *'Atiqot* ES 2 (1959), pp. 121-29; B. Landsberger and H. Tadmor, 'Fragments of Clay Liver Models from Hazor', *IEJ* 14 (1964), pp. 201-18; cf. refs. 21 and 29.

28. Cf. B.M. Gitlen, 'The Cultural and Chronological Implications of the Cypro-Palestinian Trade during the Late Bronze Age', *BASOR* 241 (1981), pp. 49-59; A. Leonard, 'Considerations of Morphological Variation in the Mycenean Pottery from the Southeastern Mediterranean', *BASOR* 241 (1981), pp. 87-101.

the radical changes that began around 1200 and led to the end of numerous city-states. Many cities such as Hazor were destroyed as early as around 1200 and not rebuilt; others, such as Lachish, disappeared from history about 1150. But there is also a stark difference visible in the places which were reoccupied in the twelfth and eleventh centuries; for example a clear break is discernible at Megiddo in the transition from Stratum VII A to Stratum VI. Even though city culture did not come to an abrupt end, there was a clear break around 1150, which can only be described as the breakdown of the system of independent city-states with their claims to power and their urban way of life. The reasons for the end of a settlement form and building tradition which had lasted for eight centuries are unknown, since written sources are largely absent.[29] In accordance with the present state of knowledge a number of factors must be assumed to have been responsible for this deurbanization:

1. Those groups identified as *ḥapiru* in Akkadian and *'prw* in Egyptian texts are known from the sources as an element of political unrest throughout the whole period.[30] These Apiru cannot be more closely categorized, but they constitute elements of lower social rank within the order of society, who are in sharp contrast to the local population and probably present a constant latent threat, even though their numbers are not sufficient for a military expedition or conquest.

2. From the reign of Merenptah (1213–1203) onwards, Egypt and with it the Egyptian province of Canaan was frequently under threat from the so-called Peoples of the Sea.[31] Ramses III won a decisive victory over these enemies in a double battle on land and at sea in 1176, and thus averted the threat posed by

---

29. There is an inventory of all the cuneiform texts found in the country in Galling, *Textbuch zur Geschichte Israels*, pp. 13-14. The most important new discovery is mentioned in D.L. Owen, 'An Akkadian Letter from Ugarit at Tell Aphek', *Tel Aviv* 8 (1981), pp. 1-17.

30. On the Apiru cf. the summary presented by O. Loretz, *Habiru-Hebräer* (BZAW 160; 1984).

31. On the Peoples from the Sea cf. G.A. Lehmann, 'Der Untergang des hethitischen Großreiches und die neuen Texte aus Ugarit', *UF* 2 (1970), pp. 39-73; G.A. Lehmann, 'Die "Seevölker"-Herrschaften an der Levanteküste', in *Jahresbericht des Instituts für Vorgeschichte der Universität Frankfurt a. M.* (1976, 1977), pp. 78-111; R. Stadelmann, 'Die Abwehr der Seevölker unter Ramses III', *Saeculum* 19 (1968), pp. 156-71.

them. The sources are silent about the possible havoc which preceded this final subjugation. In view of the danger for the New Kingdom which emanated from this migrational movement it can certainly be assumed that the Peoples of the Sea contributed to the destruction of Canaanite cities.

3. The countless campaigns carried out by the Pharaohs and the wars between the cities could have brought about a decline in the population and a weakening of the economic foundation.
4. Factors still unknown, such as long dry periods or leaching of the soil, could have led to the final abandonment of many cities.

The extent to which the break-up of the Mycenaean world around 1200 affected the Canaanite cities is beyond our knowledge. At any rate, trade with the Aegean was brought broadly to a standstill, a fact also documented by the complete cessation of the flow of those imported ceramics which attest to far-reaching and intensive relations in the Late Bronze Age. After the reign of Ramses III (1184–1153) the Egyptian hegemony over Canaan collapsed, and only sporadic monuments to the later Ramessids have been found. The visible break in the history of urbanization around 1150 is consistent with an upheaval in political circumstances.

Life after the Breakdown

Some cities continued to exist even after the collapse of the Canaanite system of rule around 1150. The continuity of the settlement history until the end of the eleventh century at some Late Bronze Age sites points to the ongoing existence of the Canaanite population. However, as is shown by the settlement in Megiddo Stratum VI A, a further decline in the culture is obvious; a surrounding wall is missing, and temple and palace were not rebuilt (fig. 8). Yet particular elements are retained. Apparently, a certain protection was aimed for through the closed, built-up nature of the outer limit of the site. (The conclusions here are not clear, since severe destruction was caused by the building of the city wall in Iron Age II.) Access was at that place on the northern boundary where the gate had been situated since Middle Bronze Age II A, though here only two small towers were built to flank the entrance, instead of a solid gate construction. There were public buildings on both sides of the gateway; the former were far behind the Late Bronze Age palaces in terms of size, but are still indications of the continuation of central rule and administration. Domestic architecture in the eastern and southern sectors is extremely badly preserved, so that building forms and the layout of the streets cannot be discerned. As the previous division into *insulae* is no longer apparent, it seems that building operations were carried on without a planned concept. Even though the temple was not immediately rebuilt, the existence of a cultic place in another location cannot be excluded since large areas of the city have not yet been excavated. Megiddo retained the character of a city in Stratum VI A, although the buildings used for government and for cultic practices were greatly reduced in number; thus this level can most accurately be described as a domestic settlement still inhabited by Canaanites.

Figure 11. *Beth-Shean. City of Stratum V.*

A certain inertia after 1150 is also exhibited by Beth-Shean in Stratum V (fig. 11), which represents the city until the end of the eleventh century.[32] Although the division into *insulae* recognizable in Stratum VI

32. F.W. James, *The Iron Age at Beth Shan* (1966), pp. 30-45 and Fig. 75. The role of Beth-Shan in the death of Saul in 1 Samuel 31, pp. 8-13 does not make it necessary to speak of the city of Stratum V as Philistine.

is not retained, the aim of forming closed complexes is clearly visible.[33] Two temples with comprehensive outbuildings were built on the site of their predecessors, though the ground plan was considerably altered. Thus two long-room temples with nonaxially orientated entrances were formed out of the Egyptian type with broad-room cella and raised adyton. The building form of the Egyptian private house disappeared in the adjoining residential area to the north. Even though the dividing lines between the individual private houses can only be distinguished with difficulty, the tendency to form a closed built-up unit is unmistakable.

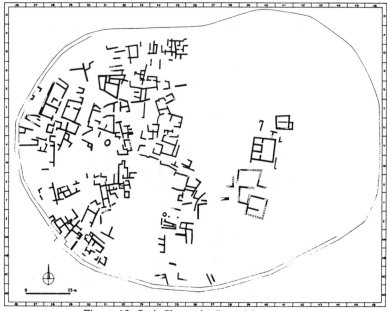

Figure 12. *Beth-Shemesh. City of Stratum III.*

In Beth-Shemesh, the Early Iron Age city (Stratum III) cannot be completely separated from that of the period of the monarchy (Stratum II) (fig. 12).[34] As in Megiddo Stratum VI A, there was apparently no longer a city wall. The houses are close together without any underlying principle of order; they form an agglomeration, without a pattern of streets being visible. Although for the most part only the western half of the city has been uncovered, no different pattern of building is to be assumed

33. The stratigraphical and chronological problems have not even been solved by further excavations which were carried out in 1982. Cf. Y. Yadin and Sh. Geva, 'Investigations at Beth Shean. The Early Iron Age Strata' (Qedem 23; 1986).

34. E. Grant, *Rumeileh being 'Ain Shems Excavations III* (1934), map II.

for the eastern half. As there is a widespread absence of complete ground plans, nothing can be said about the types of house that existed there, but the larger unwalled sectors must be thought of as courts. Here also, where various built units crowd one another, no unity of building construction was achieved, and incoherent juxtaposition predominates, rather as in the southern quarter of Megiddo Stratum VI A. On the basis of the Philistine pottery the city can be dated from the mid-twelfth to the mid-eleventh century. Since the high percentage of Philistine-type wares can be explained by the fact that the city is a neighbour to the Philistine cities of Ekron and Gat, Beth-Shemesh Stratum III should not be counted as part of the area under the power of the Philistine Pentapolis but can be considered as the successor of the former Canaanite city.

New cities were also founded during Iron Age I, as is demonstrated by the city on *Tell Qasīle*.[35] Although nothing can be said about the layout of the city in Strata XII and XI during the second half of the twelfth and first half of the eleventh centuries, orderly planning is visible in Stratum X which dates from the second half of the eleventh century (fig. 13). The city was surrounded by a wall, the existence of which has been demonstrated on the western side; the position of the city gate is unknown. In spite of certain differences in ground plan, the houses are set together in the form of *insulae*. Because of the projecting and recessed sections of individual buildings, no strict building line results but the streets run in more or less straight lines so that they cross each other at right angles. Three- and four-room houses predominate among the types of construction, but the existence of a pillar-house has also been demonstrated. The temple in the north-east quarter is difficult to categorize, consisting as it does of a vestibule, the cella, and a room situated at the back of the latter. The roof was held up by two central supports. This long-room building was preceded by two almost rectangular cultic buildings of smaller size in Strata XII and XI. This temple has no parallels in the Canaanite culture; various elements point, however, to a connection with the Aegean, without a derivation from the realm of Mycenaean culture being either possible or imperative.[36]

35. Cf. B. Maisler, 'The Excavations at Tell Qasile. Preliminary Report', *IEJ* 1 (1950-1), pp. 61-83, 125-40, 194-218; A. Mazar, 'Excavations at Tell Qasile I/II' (Qedem 12 and 20; 1980 and 1985); *idem*, 'Excavations at Tell Qasile, 1982-1984; Preliminary Report', *IEJ* 36 (1986), pp. 1-15.

36. J. Schäfer, 'Bemerkungen zum Verhältnis mykenischer Kultbauten zu Tempelbauten in Kanaan', *Archäologischer Anzeiger* (1983), pp. 551-58.

The occupation layer in Stratum X thus presents a complex picture.
The city is a successor to the Philistine-type foundations of Strata XII and
XI, which are characterized by Philistine pottery; a change in the nature of
the population is not to be reckoned with here. The layout of the site
exhibits the careful execution of the elements that were customary in the
Canaanite cities during the Late Bronze Age. These were fortification by
means of a city wall, a system of streets at right-angles to one another and
the formation of *insulae* through the positioning together of houses
and other buildings. The forms of construction used, however, do not

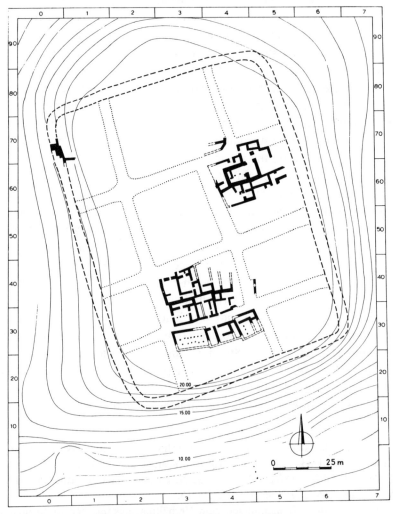

Figure 13. Tell Qasīle. *City of Stratum X.*

correspond to that of the Canaanite courtyard house, but present an innovation that is then typical of the Early Iron Age settlements (cf. Chapter 4). An explanation for this mixture of different traditions has yet to be given.

With the exception of the new foundation on *Tell Qasīle*, there is no unified picture of the continuity of settlement history after the Canaanite cities of the Late Bronze Age. On the one hand, a clear preservation of the building tradition, as for example at Beth-Shean, can be discerned. On the other hand however, in Megiddo Stratum VI A and Beth-Shemesh Stratum III, the signs of a strong deurbanization are unmistakable. In spite of the clear break which occurred with the collapse of the Canaanite city-states around 1150, the phenomenon of the city does not simply disappear from history.

Chapter 4

THE EARLY IRON AGE SETTLEMENTS

Some cities continued to exist in more modest form even after the final collapse of the Canaanite city states during the twelfth century. A certain continuity is shown in Megiddo Stratum VI A, although the gate and the palace no longer exhibit their previous size and there was no longer a temple. Other urban centres continued to exist, particularly on the coastal plain; these were built on the ruins of the Late Bronze Age cities.

Apart from the Philistine cities of Ashdod, Ekron and Gat, the Canaanite culture continued on at Timna, Gezer, Jaffa and on *Tell Jerīshe* during the twelfth and eleventh centuries.[1] There was even a new foundation on *Tell el-Qasīle*, which exhibits all the characteristics of Canaanite city planning. The tradition of city building, as it had existed for centuries, was thus further preserved in the coastal plain, even though there was also a continuation of settlement history in numerous locations in the remaining parts of Palestine, as has been demonstrated at Megiddo, Beth-Shean and Beth-Shemesh (cf. above Chapter 3). A number of cities were not rebuilt after their destruction, but lay in ruins, such as for example Taanach and Lachish, until the new urbanization of the Iron Age which began in the tenth century. Yet the tradition of urban culture was perpetuated to a certain degree in the settlements that succeeded the former Canaanite centres, although it no longer manifested itself in its full form.

Parallel to this deurbanization the number of nonurban settlements in

---

1. On Timna cf. G.L. Kelm and A. Mazar, 'Tel Batash (Timnah) Excavations: Second Preliminary Report (1981-2)', *BASOR Supplement* 23 (1985), pp. 93-120; on Gezer cf. W.G. Dever (ed.), *Gezer II: Report of the 1967-70 seasons in Fields I and II* (1974), and *Gezer IV: The 1969-71 seasons in Field VI, the 'Acropolis'* (1986); on Jaffa cf. J. Kaplan, 'The Archaeology and History of Tel Aviv-Jaffa', *BA* 35 (1972), pp. 66-95; on *Tell Jerīshe* cf. S. Geva, *Excavations at Tell Jerishe* (Qedem 15; 1982).

Palestine increased notably. These villages, newly-founded during the twelfth and eleventh centuries, lie mostly outside the vicinity of the former urban centres or in areas which had not been settled at all during the Middle and Late Bronze Ages. Thus the existence of these new foundations has been demonstrated in particular in the mountains of Galilee, Ephraim and Judaea, in the Transjordan and in the Negev; in these places the history of the settlement can be subject to strong regional variations.[2] Most of the villages are relatively small, with an area of 0.5–1 hectares (1.25–2.5 acres). Their large number however, necessitated a completely altered settlement structure. Instead of the few urban centres which held sway over the respective surrounding area through deployment of their power, the country is now covered by small villages, which subsist through the cultivation of fields and meadowland in the immediate vicinity.

The few excavated sites allow recognition of a certain variety in layout and in building forms. They were mostly founded in places without any previous history, but they could also, as in the case of Ai, be built on ruins dating from the Early Bronze Age or on the ruined tells of deserted Canaanite cities, as at Hazor. In most cases they were abandoned after the beginning of urbanization in the tenth century, as it is only in exceptional cases, such as at *Tell es-Seba'*, that the city of the period of the monarchy stands upon the remains of a village from the Early Iron Age. This type of agricultural settlement is thus an extraordinary phenomenon, requiring explanation, during which detailed discussion of the controversial questions concerning the ethnic affiliations of the inhabitants and historical development must be put aside. Of more importance here is a closer characterization of the settlements that have been excavated. For this purpose, only sites of which adequate areas have been studied by excavation will be taken into account. The sites are dated on the basis of the ceramic chronology. Since however the pottery exhibits an unbroken continuity in the period between 1150 and 1000 and the transitions between the adjoining periods are not sharply defined, the dates mentioned can only be used as points for orientation and a leeway of from two to three decades must be taken into account. As a whole, however, the chronology is well secured because of an equation of the ceramics with datable Egyptian finds.

---

2. All of the sites known through surface examination are evaluated in I. Finkelstein, *The Archaeology of the Israelite Settlement* (1988).

Hazor

After the destruction of the Canaanite city the site remained uninhabited
for a certain period. During the course of the twelfth and eleventh
centuries there were two settlements on the tell, each of which only
lasted for a short period of time.[3] These two Strata XII and XI are of an
extremely poor character and do not represent any continuation of the
former city. The minimal extent of the areas which have been excavated
does not permit any far-reaching observations to be made. Stratum XII
boasts only modest remains in the form of foundation walls, ovens and
storage pits. A building with a row of the stone pillars typical of the
period was located in Stratum XI; although the ground plan cannot be
fully ascertained, this is in no way to be designated as a cultic building.
The extent of the area covered by this occupation layer cannot yet be
established, but it must with relative certainty have consisted only of an
unfortified village of minimal size.

Tell Qiri

Tell Qiri lies about 9 km north west of Megiddo on the edge of the
Plain of Jesreel; the old name of the settlement is unknown. The Early
Iron Age village was built upon the remains of a city of Middle Bronze
Age II A, which had already been abandoned during the Middle Bronze
Age II B period.[4] The history of the settlement subsequently carries on
down into the Hellenistic and Roman period, with only a short break,
but the place was never fortified.

Two occupation layers which date to the twelfth and eleventh centuries have been identified in Strata IX and VIII, though each of these is
to be subdivided into three phases on account of the frequent building
activity which took place there. These phases exhibit considerable diver-
gences in building style. In Stratum VIII C the houses form a closely
interlocking pattern, and two of them are of the three-room house type.
In Stratum VIII B the same sector produced a row of almost square
houses, which were divided internally into one wide room and a courtyard area by means of a cross-wall or a row of stone pillars. In one

3. Cf. Y. Yadin, *Hazor* (1972), pp. 129-34.
4. A. Ben-Tor and Y. Portugali, *Tell Qiri. A Village in the Jezreel Valley*
(Qedem 24; 1987).

house, a further room had been built on the side of the house opposite the entrance, so that the resulting plan is that of a three-room house. In the following phase, Stratum VIII A, the building form of the broad-room house with courtyard area is retained, but the position of the houses in relation to one another was changed once again, although numerous walls were re-used. The course followed by the streets was not taken into account here; thus the streets did not represent insurmountable limitations where building operations were concerned.

Because of the limited nature of the area which has been excavated, nothing can be said about the layout of the village. The completely irregular pattern of streets does not allow recognition of any planning; the only concern here was with access to the houses. Various basic types could be employed side by side in domestic construction; these were not arranged next to each other in a recognizable order, but in an 'interlocking' pattern and thus each house provided its own border with the next. The large number of the forms of construction is worthy of note; apart from broad-room houses with courtyards extending in front of them there was also the so-called three-room house and the type of house which was subdivided along its length by means of stone pillars.

Shilo

As the sources reveal, Shilo played an important role in the premonarchical period, since it is here that the Ark of the Covenant was kept until it was lost to the Philistines (cf. 1 Sam. 1–4). As far as the Early Iron Age settlement is concerned, only a few houses on the western edge of the mound have been excavated to date;[5] these had been set into the *glacis* of the Middle Bronze Age fortifications (fig. 14). Because of this, the houses do not conform to any of the usual types, but they do, however, contain the stone pillars that are typical of the period, which served to subdivide what were relatively large building units. Those houses further down the slope were given stability by supporting walls, thus creating cellar rooms which, as the numerous pithoi found there suggest, were used for storage purposes. The village only existed for a short period, from the end of the twelfth until the middle of the eleventh century.

5.   Sh. Bunimovitz, 'Excavations at Shiloh 1981-84: Preliminary Report 2. Area C: The Iron Age I Buildings and other Remains', *Tel Aviv* 12 (1985), pp. 130-39.

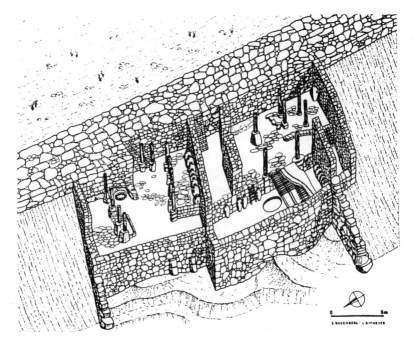

Figure 14. *Shiloh. Reconstruction of houses of Iron Age I.*

Ai

Ai lies on the hill called *et-Tell* on the southern edge of the *Wādi el-Jaya*, about 5 km east of Ramallah in the neighbourhood of Beth-El, with *Bētīn* only 3 km further to the west. The Early Iron Age settlement (fig. 15) was established on the acropolis of the Early Bronze Age city, which once extended over an area of 11 hectares (*c*. 27.5 acres) on a hill sloping down to the east.[6] It seems that the city wall dating from the third millennium was still visible, but no attempt was made to make use of it. By contrast, the Early Bronze Age broad-room temple was furnished with partition walls and used as a habitation. The wide area of the hill was not taken into account, and the houses were closely packed together into an area of about 1 hectare (*c*. 2.5 acres). Predominant is the long, extended type of private house, in which the main room is mostly subdivided by means of stone pillars; a further room is divided

---

6. Cf. the preliminary report by J.A. Callaway, 'Ai', *NEAEHL* I (1993), pp. 39-45.

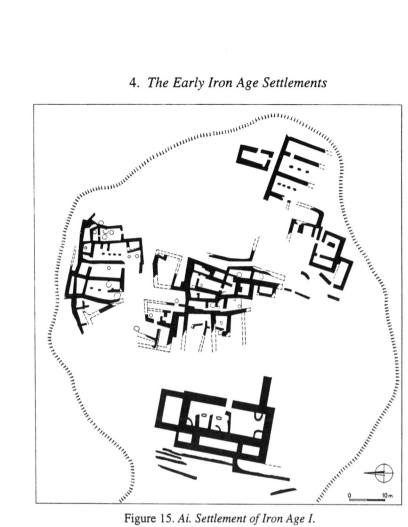

Figure 15. *Ai. Settlement of Iron Age I.*

off on the narrow side, which is opposite the entrance. Smaller, rectangular rooms are located singly. Occasionally, two rooms were connected
with each other by low passageways. The houses exhibit considerable
variations in size. On the northern edge of the village complex the
houses were built next to each other in such a way that the external
walls present an unbroken facade; thus a certain defensive posture is
achieved. The water storage cisterns in which rainwater was collected
were located inside the houses. These cisterns were bell-shaped and
hewn out of the limestone of the hill, so that no further sealing through
the application of a coating to the walls was necessary.

The extremely irregular method of building is conspicuous, particularly
in the northern quarter. An alleyway seems to have run between here
and the built-up area in the centre, but not in a straight line. An irregular
course of the streets is also recognizable at the eastern edge of the
central built-up area. Public buildings are absent, and what was once the

temple is subdivided by means of partition walls and used as a place of dwelling. Numerous storage silos attest to the agricultural character of the settlement. The practice of animal husbandry is indicated by finds of bones but the herds of sheep and goats were kept outside the residential settlement. The village was founded around 1200 and continued in existence until about 1050; two phases of building can be discerned during this period. In the second phase, after 1150, room was made to accommodate a larger number of inhabitants by means of additional buildings and partition walls. This also necessitated an increase in the number of storage silos. There is, however, nothing to indicate that a change took place where the identity of the inhabitants is concerned. The reasons why the village was abandoned cannot be established.

In *Khirbet Raddāne*, immediately to the north-west of Ramallah, large parts of a village have been excavated which must have been about contemporary with Ai. A plan of the village has yet to be published. In contrast to Ai, the houses were constructed in a very regular manner based on the plan of the so-called three-room house; they largely follow a uniform orientation from east to west.[7] Further details are at present unknown.

Khirbet ed-Dawwara

The small village of *Khirbet ed-Dawwara* is situated to the north of Jerusalem in the territory of the tribe of Benjamin. It only covers an area of 0.5 hectares (*c.* 1.25 acres) and its ancient name is unknown.[8] The settlement was surrounded by a solid wall, the width of which varied between 2 and 3 m. Three houses were excavated on the west side which, although they were not completely preserved, can be reconstructed as four-room houses (fig. 16). Their varying methods of construction are worthy of note: the back rooms of two of these houses abut onto the encircling wall, while one of them was set parallel to it. The village seems to have been founded towards the end of the eleventh century and existed for a certain length of time down into the tenth century. The solid wall indicates the transition to a fortified city, without

7. J.A. Callaway and R.E. Cooley, 'A Salvage Excavation at Raddana in Bireh', *BASOR* 201 (1971), pp. 9-19. An Early Iron Age village has also been discovered at Bet-El, cf. J.L. Kelso, *The Excavations of Bethel (1934-1960)* (AASOR 39; 1968).

8. Finkelstein, *Israelite Settlement*, pp. 262-63 with figure 86 and *IEJ* 38 (1988), pp. 79-80.

a meaningful arrangement of the houses having been achieved when building took place within the walls. In every instance, the protective encircling wall was constructed together with the private houses. This settlement thus represents a connecting link between the Early Iron Age village structure and the urbanization which set in during the period of the monarchy.

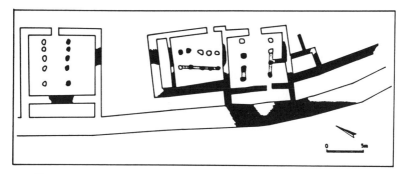

Figure 16. Khirbet ed-Dawwara. *Houses and wall of the 11th c. BC.*

Gīlōh

Gīlōh is a name selected arbitrarily for a village located about 2 km to the north of *Bēt Jalā* in the Judaean Mountains. Apart from buildings dating from the period of the monarchy, the remains of a small settlement which existed for a few decades around 1200 were discovered there.[9] Three imperfectly preserved houses have been excavated at this settlement, together with long sections of widely-extending encircling walls which closed off larger areas (fig.17). It is likely that these walls were intended less for the protection of the inhabitants than for the accommodation of animals. The bad state of preservation makes reconstruction of the buildings just as impossible as the exact establishment of the limits of the animal corrals. This was apparently not a village settlement but rather a collection of farmsteads, probably with animal husbandry as the main occupation.

ʿIzbet Ṣarṭah

The name *ʿIzbet Ṣarṭah* is given to a village established on the eastern edge of the Ephraim Mountains, on the Heights of Afek. A village was

9.   A. Mazar, 'Giloh: An Early Israelite Settlement Site near Jerusalem', *IEJ* 31 (1981), pp. 1-36.

founded after 1200 in a hitherto unsettled location, and this continued to
exist, in three layers of occupation, until down into the tenth century.[10]
In the oldest settlement of Stratum III a row of broad rooms was
discovered in each of two locations opposite one another; these rooms
can be construed as having formed part of a settlement with an oval
layout (fig. 18). The rooms, arranged in a ring formation, surround a
large, open area, in which the existence of several silos could be
established. The reconstruction of this village to form an enclosed

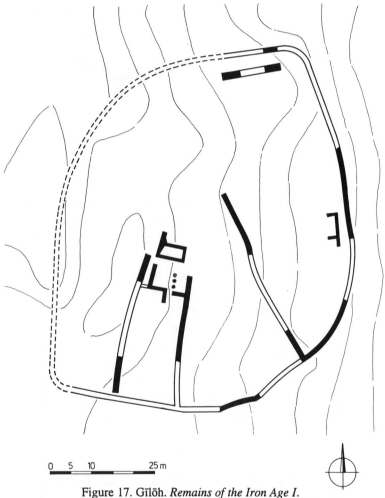

0   5   10   25 m

Figure 17. Gīlōh. *Remains of the Iron Age I.*

10. Finkelstein, *Israelite Settlement*, pp. 73-80.

precinct is supported by the fact that similar layouts have been found in the Negev; however, the latter are only to be dated to the tenth century and should therefore not be brought forward as a contemporary parallel.[11]

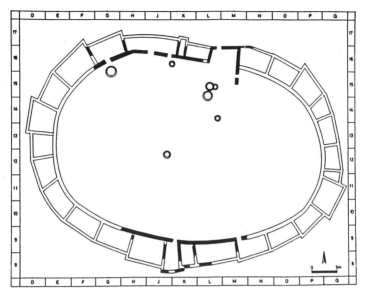

Figure 18. 'Izbet Ṣarṭah. *Reconstruction of the settlement in Stratum III.*

The organization into a closed oval is clearly functional in purpose, since it offers a certain protection against attack. Even though the possibilities for defence were limited, a surprise incursion was out of the question. The similarity of this form of settlement to the camp arrangement of the Bedouin, whose tents are erected around a central area, cannot lead to the conclusion that this form of settlement was taken over from a nomadic form of life and thus attests to the transition of people not permanently settled to a state of permanent settlement.[12] At any rate, it can be presumed that animals could also be accommodated inside the settlement, if this became necessary. From the layout this was more likely an enclosure than a village.

Towards the end of the eleventh century, a new settlement with a completely different character was built (Stratum II). Apart from a row of houses containing two rows of stone pillars there were different types

11. R. Cohen, 'The Iron Age Fortresses in the Central Negev', *BASOR* 226 (1979), pp. 61-79.

12. Contra Finkelstein, *Israelite Settlement*, pp. 238-50.

of outbuildings of varying dimensions (fig. 19). The largest of these houses measured 16 × 12 m and is further subdivided by means of a crosswall, so that it exhibits the plan of a four-room house. In the case of this house, the entrance is situated in one corner of the long side. Although all the houses are orientated in an approximate north-south direction, no planning of any kind is recognizable. Numerous silos for storage are to be found in their vicinity. The place was unfortified and can only have existed for two or three decades.

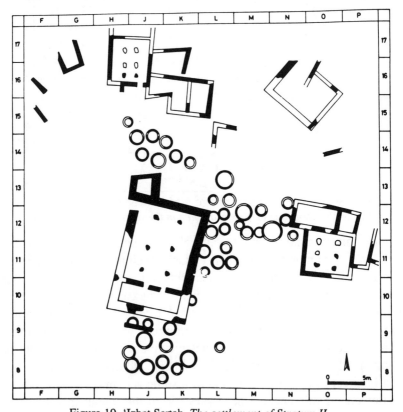

Figure 19. 'Izbet Ṣarṭah. *The settlement of Stratum II.*

Tell es-Seba'

The history of the settlement on *Tell es-Seba'* begins in the second half of the twelfth century and continues in an unbroken sequence down to the end of the eighth century. The foundation of the fortified city of Stratum V is preceded by a total of four settlement layers, which all

have a village-like character but exhibit strong deviations of layout.[13]
The oldest settlement in Stratum IX is limited to inhabited pits on the
south-eastern slope of the natural hill to the north of *Wādi es-Seba'*.
These inhabited pits were at least partly roofed-over, with a width of up
to 12 m. It is probable that they were occupied by members of a
nomadic society over a long period of more than one hundred years.

The building of permanent houses only began in Stratum VIII, when
permanent habitation finally became a reality. The transition to house
building took place in the middle of the eleventh century, but the
remains are extremely scanty because the settlement was largely
destroyed by the building which took place during Stratum VII. Only
the form of one building can be determined with any certainty; in the
straight course of its walls it attests to the adoption of a developed form
of construction, a broad room with a court in front of it. A silo was situated outside the north-eastern corner. Some of the pits from Stratum IX
were probably also put to further use.

Only very sparse remains were found of the settlement in Stratum VII,
which was a new foundation in the last quarter of the eleventh century
(fig. 20). The reconstruction of the individual house units remains
hypothetical. Entrance to the village was between two tower-like, free-
standing buildings. More houses lay outside this ring of houses. The
reconstruction of the place as a precinct with an open area enclosed by a
ring of houses, as put forward by Z. Herzog, is by no means certain.[14]
The arrangement of the houses to form an unbroken external façade in
this way is certainly demonstrated at Ai, but there dense building had
taken place throughout the whole area covered by the settlement (cf.
fig. 15). In the corral-like layout at *'Izbet Ṣarṭah* Stratum III the outer
ring consists of only simple broad rooms (cf. fig. 18). Thus the concept
of the closed settlement cannot summarily be applied in the case of other
locations.

13. Z. Herzog, *Beer-sheba II. The Early Iron Age Settlements* (1984). The old
name of the place is unknown. The identification with the biblical Beersheba by
Y. Aharoni, *Beersheba*, I (1973), p. 1 is by no means certain, since the latter can be
placed in the area of *Bir es-Seba'* a few km to the west of *Tell es-Seba'*.

14. Z. Herzog, *Beersheba*, II, Figs. 34 and 35.

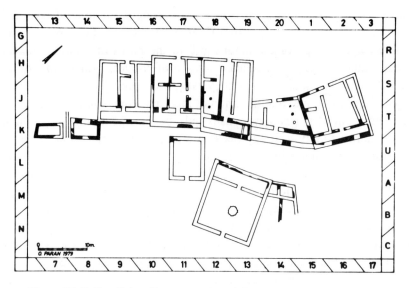

Figure 20. Tell es-Seba'. *Reconstruction of the settlement in Stratum VII.*

After the destruction which took place around 1000 a new settlement was built once more in Stratum VI, to be replaced by a fortified city during the first half of the tenth century. As in the case of Stratum VII, the existence of a number of houses set side by side in rows could be determined, but these were not constructed according to a uniform plan (fig. 21). The three-room house is represented here, with one room separated off by means of stone pillars and a room on the narrow side, while the rest of the domestic buildings differ from each other to a greater or lesser degree and do not allow recognition of a uniform ground plan.

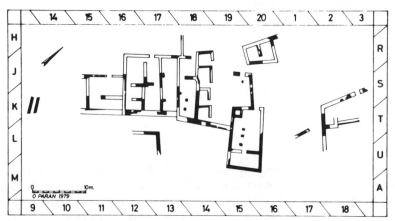

Figure 21. Tell es-Seba'. *The settlement of Stratum XII.*

Arad

Even before the construction of a fortress in the tenth century, a small village existed during the eleventh century in Arad Stratum XII (fig. 22); its extent cannot however be established, as it was partly destroyed by later overbuilding.[15] The remains are accordingly sparse and consist for the most part of a few, only partly preserved houses, several silos outside the residential area and a large paved square with the remains of a semicircular structure made of mud bricks. Some of the houses have wide rooms, one is divided up by built-in stone pillars, a construction which is otherwise typical of the period. Y. Aharoni has interpreted the large square with the mud-brick structure as a cultic place;[16] this interpretation is not conclusive, however. First, no cult objects have been found, and secondly an open area inside the settlement could have served other purposes. The semicircular mud-brick structure was most likely part of a large silo. The village was surrounded by a wall, which ran along beside the houses.

Tēl ʿIsdār

Located about 20 km south-east of Beersheba, this village was only sporadically inhabited.[17] The houses in Stratum III date from the eleventh century and are arranged in a circle, so that they surround an open area of about 120 m in diameter. As the individual houses do not abut onto one another, no closed ring of defence is presented, although the arrangement clearly has a protective function, as is also recognizable in the case of Bedouin camps.[18]

The entire settlement consisted of more than twenty buildings. With one exception, the seven houses excavated were in extremely bad condition and only the complete ground plan of house 90 could be ascertained (fig. 23.1). This was a broad-room house measuring 12 × 6 m which was subdivided along its length into two parts of uneven width by a row of five stone pillars as well as a wall. On the narrow side to the

15. Z. Herzog, M. Aharoni, A.F. Rainey and S. Moshkovitz, 'The Israelite fortress at Arad', *BASOR* 254 (1984), pp. 1-34.

16. Y. Aharoni, 'Nothing Early and Nothing Late: Rewriting Israel's Conquest', *BA* 39 (1976), pp. 55-76, particularly p. 60.

17. M. Kochavi, 'Excavations at Tel Esdar', *ʿAtiqot* HS 5 (1969), pp. 14-48 (in Hebrew).

18. Cf. A. Musil, *The Manner and Customs of the Rwala Bedouin* (1928).

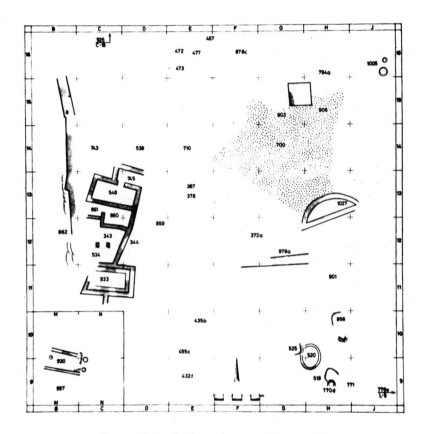

Figure 22. *Arad. The settlement of Stratum XII.*

west small rooms were divided off by cross-walls. The room in front of the row of pillars was probably not roofed over and served as a court-yard. The entire settlement was probably only inhabited for a short time.

Khirbet el-Meshâsh

The Early Iron Age settlement of *Khirbet el-Meshâsh*, whose size far exceeds that of all the other settlements of this period, is situated on the upper course of the *Wādi es-Seba'*.[19] Four occupation layers can be distinguished for the period of its existence from the beginning of the twelfth century until the beginning of the tenth century. (The further

19. V. Fritz and A. Kempinski, *Ergebnisse der Ausgrabungen auf der Hirbet el-Mšāš (Tel Māśōś) 1972-75*, I-III (1983).

subdivision of Stratum II into two phases can be disregarded, since it is only to be understood in terms of building alterations). In the oldest occupation layer, that of Stratum III B, only pits, ovens and minimal remains of walls were found, a fact which points rather to a sporadic presence of nomadic inhabitants. The actual construction of permanent houses begins in Stratum III A around the middle of the twelfth century. The only coherent building complex comprises rectangular houses with rooms on the long side and/or narrow side of the courtyard, and the use of stone pillars is demonstrated there (fig. 24.3).

The settlement reaches its greatest extent in Stratum II during the eleventh century, with an area of 3 hectares (*c.* 7.5 acres) (fig. 23). Although only a small part of the village has been excavated, the construction that had taken place on the northern and southern edges provides a good insight into its layout. In the north, several four-room houses were situated next to each other in such a way that they were accessible from the edge of the village. Thus it was not a girdle of defences that was achieved by this organization of the private houses in a row; it was rather the accessibility of fields and herds outside the settlement that was clearly of priority (fig. 25). Most of the houses are of roughly equal size, with an average of about 120 sq m. Two of the buildings are broad-room houses each with a row of pillars, but varying arrangement of the rooms. Besides these there was a building which, on the evidence of the finds made there, was used for metalworking. The buildings form straight façades, so that the streets often widen out into little squares. On the southern edge there was a building which consisted of two almost square units. The larger part contained various rooms, but the function of the building is unclear. Adjacent on the western side was a simple four-room house, which contained solid walls instead of the two rows of pillars. To the north of this complex there was an almost square building, which typologically resembles the Egyptian 'Amarna house' with its tripartite ground plan and a central living room.[20] About 30 m further to the north-west there is an example of a courtyard house, probably with a blacksmith's workshop housed in one of the rooms situated in the western part;[21] a house subdivided by stone pillars was built onto the latter.

20. V. Fritz, 'Die Verbreitung des sog. Amarna-Wohnhauses in Kanaan', *Damaszener Mitteilungen* 3 (1988), pp. 27-34.
21. Cf. V. Fritz, 'Eine Metallwerkstatt der frühen Eisenzeit (1200–1000 v. Chr.) auf der Hirbet el-Mšāš im Negeb', *Der Anschnitt, Beiheft* 7 (1989), pp. 223-26.

Thus the building that has taken place in Stratum II is extremely complex in nature. Apart from the normal four-room houses and the broad-room houses there are fortress-like buildings, the Egyptian type of domestic house and examples of the courtyard house, in which the different composition of the quarters in the north and west is notable.

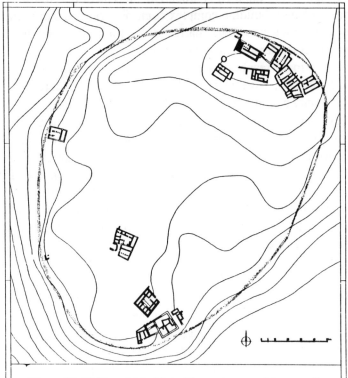

Figure 23. Khirbet el-Meshâsh. *The settlement of Stratum II.*

While the rustic private houses and the metal workshops are to be expected in a large village, the remaining buildings on the southern edge tend to present a rather puzzling aspect. In particular, the private house in Egyptian style points to a possible special position of its inhabitants in respect of race and social status, without a closer verification being possible.

Its size and the differentiation among building types there distinguishes this large village on *Khirbet el-Meshâsh* from the other settlements of the period, whose character was determined wholly by an economy based on agriculture and animal husbandry. The different types of building indicate a social and therefore also an economic differentiation, even though the majority of the inhabitants were engaged in agriculture. This recognition of an organized structure amongst the population is in agreement with the wide-ranging contacts attested to by the imported ceramics. These include Egyptian, Midianite, Philistine and Phoenician wares. The connections enjoyed by the settlement must thus have reached far into north-west Arabia and to the Phoenician coastal cities.

Because of the considerable destruction caused by erosion, Stratum I is very badly preserved; however, the existence of some four-room houses has been demonstrated. Furthermore there was a small fort on the southern edge. The settlement was abandoned shortly after 1000; the reason for this is probably to be found in the urbanization which set in anew at the beginning of the period of the monarchy.

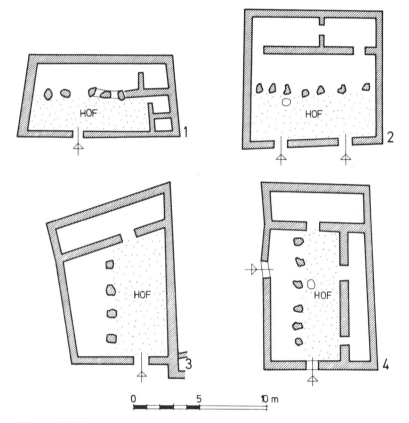

Figure 24. *Types of houses in Iron Age I. 1. Broad-room house* (Tēl 'Isdār*).
2. Broad-room house* (Khirbet el-Meshâsh *Stratum II*). *3. Three-room house* (Khirbet el-Meshâsh *Stratum III*). *4. Four-room house* (Khirbet el-Meshâsh *Stratum II*).

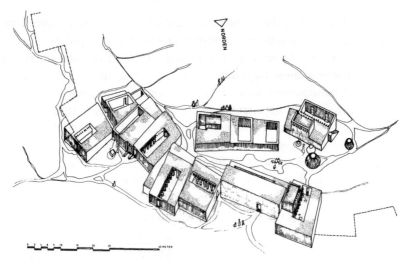

Figure 25. Khirbet el-Meshâsh. *Reconstruction of houses at the northern edge of the settlement in Stratum II*

The Forms of Settlement

The Early Iron Age settlements exhibit considerable differences in size and layout. A common feature, however, is the absence of actual monumental buildings. The palaces or temples which were a considerable component of the Canaanite city are not to be found there. As a rule the sites are unfortified, although occasionally the houses situated on the edge of the settlement are set out in the manner of a defensive ring. The first walls to provide a protective ring around the settlement only appear towards the end of the eleventh century in *Khirbet ed-Dawwara* and Arad Stratum XII. Distinguishing features of the settlements are a comparatively unordered manner of building and also the situation of numerous silos and water-storage cisterns. The houses there are by no means uniform in type. The pattern of the streets is irregular, and sometimes an open area could be left inside the settlement. Most of these villages were established in hitherto unoccupied locations, but sometimes they were built upon ruins on sites which had been abandoned long beforehand.

Along with the settlements which succeeded the Canaanite cities and which, especially in the plains, carried on the former urban tradition to a certain degree, they represent a separate element which differs considerably from the previous city culture. All the settlements have a clearly agricultural character. The inhabitants worked the surrounding land and carried on animal husbandry; here, in addition to sheep and goats there was a considerable proportion of beef cattle. The form of the economy and the number of inhabitar.ts determine the form of settlement, which could easily change from level to level.

In spite of the great variety and without the size being taken into account, at least three different types of settlement can be discerned:

1. *Ring-shaped Villages*
Characteristic of the ring-shaped village is the organization of the houses into a closed circle or oval, so that an open area remains in the middle. These houses can either be individually situated as on *Tēl 'Isdār*, or form a closed ring as in *'Izbet Sarṭah* Stratum III. Possibly the settlement at Arad in Stratum XII can also be reconstructed in this way. Through building the houses adjacent to one another the defensibility of the settlement increased. The type of house is a factor of subordinate importance, since all types are suitable for such an arrangement. Thus in *Izbet Sarṭah* Stratum III simple broad-room houses were set out in rows next to one another, while on *Tell es-Seba'* Stratum VII the four-room type predominated. The ring-shaped village corresponds to the shape of the Bedouin camp, in which the tents are grouped around an open area. Apart from the defensive function, this shape is determined by the common use of the area enclosed; here, the provision of a place of shelter for animals is the most likely function.

2. *Agglomerated Villages*
Typical of this form of settlement is the indiscriminate construction that has taken place on the site, in the form of individual buildings or complexes consisting of several houses. Streets of varying width and irregular open areas or squares are left between the individual units. The houses were positioned without planning of any kind, in accordance with the agglomerated way of building, and the edge of the village is left open. This settlement form can be assigned to the settlements at Ai, at *Khirbet Raddāne, 'Izbet Sarṭah* Stratum II, *Khirbet el-Meshâsh* Stratum II and on *Tell es-Seba'* Stratum VI. The inhabitants lived at close quarters in a comparatively restricted space and worked the fields situated outside the village. Communally used facilities could likewise have been located outside the village.

3. *Farmsteads*

The term 'farmstead' refers to single buildings or to a group of buildings surrounded by a widely-extending wall. This wall did not serve a defensive purpose but probably formed an enclosure for domestic animals. The farmstead can consist of several buildings which were erected in the vicinity of the main building as economic need dictated. The best example of such a farmstead is the settlement at *Gīlōh*.

While the existence of buildings constructed for a ruler or a central administration is not to be expected as a matter of course inside the settlements, the absence of cultic places is conspicuous. Possibly religious shrines are to be reckoned with outside the settlements, but the existence of such has not been demonstrated to date. The cultic interpretation assigned to a site enclosed by an encircling wall on the northern edge of the mountains of central Palestine is based solely on the chance find of a bronze bull figurine. It is not possible to take this small figurine alone as constituting evidence for the practice of cult; it might have been deposited there for other reasons, or have been lost there accidentally.[22] The wall could also have formed a corral for the shelter of domestic animals or enclosed a threshing floor. The remains dating from Iron Age I which have been discovered on Mount Ebal also belong to a farmstead and not to buildings designed for the practice of cult.[23] They are the remains of an agricultural holding surrounded by widely-extending walls, and their nature can be understood by analogy with the farmstead at *Gīlōh*; in a second phase of building a tower was built on top of the site. From its ground plan and features, the building described as a religious sanctuary on *Tell el-Mazār* in the Jordan Valley also served no cultic function.[24]

The layout of the settlements only allows very limited conclusions to be drawn about the inhabitants. In some places, such as *Khirbet el-Meshâsh* or *Tell es-Seba'* the building of permanent houses is preceded

22. Contra A. Mazar, 'The "Bull Site"-An Iron Age I Open Cult Place', *BASOR* 247 (1982), pp. 27-42. The interpretation is accepted without critical appraisal by R. Wenning and E. Zenger, 'Ein bäuerliches Baal-Heiligtum im samarischen Gebirge aus der Zeit der Anfänge Israels', *ZDPV* 102 (1986), pp. 75-86.

23. A. Zertal, 'An Early Iron Age Cultic Site on Mount Ebal: Excavation Seasons 1982-7', *Tel Aviv* 13-14 (1986-7), pp. 105-65. The reconstruction as the altar of Joshua is based on pure fantasy, cf. A. Kempinski, 'Joshua's Altar—An Iron Age I Watchtower', *BARev* 12.1 (1986), pp. 42-49.

24. Cf. K. Yassine, 'The Open Court Sanctuary of the Iron Age I *Tell el-Mazar* Mound A', *ZDPV* 100 (1984), pp. 108-18.

by a phase in which nomads probably constructed a camp which was used only for a short period of time. Only two groups can be considered as possible inhabitants of the new villages—Canaanites from the former cities or nomads who once lived in areas outside the cities. The supposition that the inhabitants were new immigrants is to be discounted, because the material culture clearly follows Canaanite tradition. The possibility cannot be excluded that remnants of the urban population might have withdrawn to isolated settlements in order to secure their survival.[25] Most of the villages which have been excavated to date seem to have been founded and inhabited by population groups which had not been permanently settled up to that point in time. But it is to be assumed here that they had maintained contact with the Canaanite city states over a long period of time. The new settlers did not suddenly enter Palestine from the surrounding desert, but were already living as nomads for part of the year in a certain connection with the urban centres, having come to terms with the latter; this mode of living together is most easily described as symbiotic.[26] There are important grounds for identifying the new settlers as people who previously had not had a permanent place of residence:

1. In the biblical tradition, 'Israel' signifies a new population element, which is clearly to be distinguished from that of the Canaanites.[27] According to the oldest text dating from the eleventh century, the so-called Song of Deborah in Judges 5, the Israelites were organized in individual tribes with different names, bound to each other through a certain measure of belonging together, before a political union took place under the rule of a king in the last quarter of the eleventh century.[28]

25. In particular C.H.J. De Geus, *The Tribes of Israel* (1976); N.K. Gottwald, *The Tribes of Jahweh* (1979); and N.P. Lemche, *Early Israel* (1985), envisage a population made up of groups of lower social order from the Canaanite cities, in accordance with the work of E. Mendenhall, 'The Hebrew Conquest of Palestine', *BA* 25 (1962), pp. 66-87.

26. On the continuation of the theory of infiltration developed by A. Alt in *Die Landnahme der Israeliten in Palästina* (Kleine Schriften I; 1959), pp. 89-125, cf. V. Fritz, 'Conquest or Settlement? The Early Iron Age in Palestine', *BA* 50 (1987), pp. 84-100.

27. Cf. H.-J. Zobel, 'Das Selbstverständnis Israels nach dem Alten Testament', *ZAW* 85 (1973), pp. 281-93.

28. Cf. R. Smend, 'Jahwekrieg und Stämmebund', in *Zur ältesten Geschichte Israel* (Gesammelte Studien Band 2; 1987), pp. 116-209; B. Halpern, *The Emergence of Israel in Canaan* (1983).

2. As the sources from various regions of the ancient Near East indicate, there were always nomadic groups in the vicinity of the cities during the second millennium, living together with the latter in a certain symbiosis.[29] For Canaan and the areas of steppe bordering it to the south and east the presence of a nonpermanent element of the population is well attested by the mention of the 'Shasu' (*š'św*) in Egyptian sources dating from the time of the New Kingdom.[30]

3. With the widespread collapse of the city-states during the twelfth century the symbiosis between the various groups of the population which enjoyed different ways of life also broke down. This must have had an effect on food production and the way in which it had previously been apportioned out as a task among the population. The vital provision of grain could only be ensured through increased farming, which forced the acquisition of permanent places of residence and the transition to house building.[31]

4. The architecture of the new settlements hardly exhibits any connections with Canaanite house building, but is characterized by the building of individual house types, details of whose origin and development have yet to be ascertained.[32] This break in the building tradition permits recognition of the very fact that the new settlers did not originate from the Canaanite city-states.

---

29. Cf. summary in H. Klengel, *Zwischen Zelt und Palast* (1972).

30. The evidence has been collected in R. Giveon, *Les bédouins Shosou des documents égyptiens* (1971); for its interpretation cf. M. Weippert, 'Semitische Nomaden des zweiten Jahrtausends', *Bib* 55 (1974), pp. 265-80; W. Helck, 'Die Bedrohung Palästinas durch einwandernde Gruppen am Ende der 18. und am Anfang der 19. Dynastie', *VT* 18 (1968), pp. 472-80.

31. On the relationship between the nomadic element and the cities in an agricultural society cf. M.B. Rowton, 'Urban Autonomy in a Nomadic Environment', *JNES* 32 (1973), pp. 201-15; *idem*, 'Dimorphic Structure and the Parasocial Element', *JNES* 36 (1977), pp. 181-98; J. Henninger, *Über Lebensraum und Lebensformen der Frühsemiten* (1968).

32. Cf. the researches of Y. Shiloh, 'The Four Room House: Its Situation and Function in the Israelite City', *IEJ* 20 (1970), pp. 180-90; V. Fritz, 'Bestimmung und Herkunft des Pfeilerhauses in Israel', *ZDPV* 93 (1977), pp. 30-45; F. Braemer, *L'architecture domestique du Levant à l'âge du fer* (1982).

Forms of Building

In their layout the settlements are by no means uniform, and the types of house built are also extraordinarily varied (cf. fig. 23). Apart from numerous houses which cannot be classified as to type, the following basic forms can be distinguished:

1. Broad-room Houses

The simple broad-room form of house is only found in the ring-shaped settlement of *'Izbet Ṣarṭah* Stratum III; the free-standing houses already exhibit a more developed form, as is shown by the examples at *Tēl 'Isdār* and on *Khirbet el-Meshâsh* (cf. fig. 23: 1.2). Common characteristics are the position of the entrance on the long side and the uneven subdivision along the length by a row of pillars. Further rooms could be created by cross-walls or extensions. The question of the extent of the roofed-over area, which is decisive in the understanding of the type of house, cannot unfortunately be provided with a clear answer, since no clarification is possible as to whether the wider part of the section subdivided by stone pillars was covered over and thus constituted a room and not a court. The greater width of this unit and the absence of windows suggest the probability that this section was open, in order to supply the house with air and light. This form of the broad-room house thus differs radically from the common domestic house of the Early Bronze Age (cf. above, Chapter 2).

2. Pillar-houses

The pillar-house is relatively rare; a few examples are found in *'Izbet Ṣarṭah* Stratum II (fig. 18) and on *Khirbet el-Meshâsh* Stratum II (fig. 24). The building is divided into three units along its length by two rows of stone pillars. Of these units, the middle one is wider than the two side ones. The entrance leads into this middle part, which was not roofed-over because of its width and thus was probably a court.

3. Three-room and Four-room Houses

The term 'four-room' house denotes a building which is not only divided lengthwise by two rows of stone pillars but also has a further room in the back of it. Examples of such houses have been yielded by numerous settlements of the prestate period (cf. fig. 23.4). The nomenclature 'four-room house' is misleading, inasmuch as the central part was a courtyard, with the entrance normally leading into it. Otherwise it is actually a particular form of the courtyard house, but the common nomenclature should be retained in order to avoid misunderstandings. The basic underlying concept could be changed through a multitude of variations in the manner of building and the division into rooms. The occasional extension through annexes shows precisely that this is an established, particular type of house. The three-room house is to be considered a smaller variant of this building form, in which only one room is separated from the court (fig. 23.3).

These three forms of domestic architecture are typologically connected, but a clear derivation for them has not yet been established.[33] The Early Iron Age houses are distinguished from the Canaanite courtyard house by the use of stone pillars and by their clear room division. Although the rooms are similarly arranged around a court, the position and shape of the individual rooms are fixed in a clear and unalterable form which is not usurped even by further subdivision.

A comparison of the forms of building shows that, because of its advanced plan, the four-room house stands at the end of a special development; thus the two other forms must be of an earlier date as far as the history of building is concerned. However, the broad-room house and the pillar-house share a common characteristic in the demarcation of a court by means of stone pillars within a rectangular building; they differ from one another in the position of the court and the position of the entrance, itself determined by the former. Despite this difference, the common features point to the fact that both types originate from a common basic form, that of a house subdivided into court and semi-open rooms by the placing of pillars. The evolution of this building type can be traced back into the Late Bronze Age in individual examples,[34] but the wide distribution of the type in all its variations is first met from 1150 onwards in the Early Iron Age settlements. The variable position of the court in the different types is brought about by

33. The attempted derivation from tent building methods must thus be abandoned, cf. A. Kempinski, 'From Tent to House', in V. Fritz and A. Kempinski, *Ergebnisse der Ausgrabungen auf der Hirbet el-Mšāš (Tel Māšōš) 1972-75*, I-III (1983), pp. 31-34.

34. Although the Late Bronze Age house in Timna Stratum VII is divided lengthways by two rows of stone pillars, the entrance is on the narrow side, cf. G.L. Kelm and A. Mazar, 'Tel Batash (Timnah) Excavations. Second Preliminary Report (1981-1983)', *BASOR Supplement* 23 (1985), pp. 93-120, Fig. 8.

the necessity of access to the rooms in each respective case; this possibly reflects the differing uses to which they were put. It is probable that the three-room and four-room houses originate from the extension of the pillar-house by means of an additional room on the short wall opposite the entrance. Even if it is supposed that the pillar-house was taken over from the Canaanite building tradition, its further evolution certainly took place in the Early Iron Age settlements of the prestate period.

Chapter 5

THE CITIES IN THE PERIOD OF THE MONARCHY

After the establishment of the monarchy by Saul, there followed a wave of new city foundations under his successors David and Solomon which largely replaced the previous village-type of settlement. This reurbanization also continued during the later period of the monarchy. The building of the new cities reflected the demand made by the new state that its power be secured both outwardly and inwardly; this was a development which occupied a time lasting several generations. There were now new requirements where the location of the city was concerned, and these went over and above the prerequisites that had existed for the prestate settlements. Apart from the vital details such as the presence of a water source and agricultural land in the vicinity, the aspects of defensibility and strategic position near roads of communication, which had already been of fundamental importance to the Canaanite city, now had to be taken into consideration. Thus it is not surprising that numerous Israelite cities were newly-founded on the sites of ruined Bronze Age cities which had long since been abandoned. Such a resumption in the history of a settlement after several centuries is discernible at Dan, Hazor, *Tell el-Fār'ah*, Lachish and in numerous other places.

A differentiation is to be made between this new settlement and the takeover of those Canaanite sites which had survived the destruction after 1200 and were still fortified. These last remnants of Canaanite city culture were similarly developed into Israelite cities after their incorporation into the kingdom, as was the case at Megiddo, Gezer, Beth-Shemesh and on *Tell Beit Mirsim* and as can also be supposed in the case of the new capital, Jerusalem (cf. below, Chapter 6). Only in a few cases was the city established on the site of an Early Iron Age village, as can be seen at Kinneret and also in the city on *Tell es-Seba'*.

Only a few of the numerous cities of the Iron Age have been excavated to such an extent that their structure is discernible. In addition, the individual occupation layers were not adequately separated out from one another during the excavations that took place in the first decades of archaeological research, so that no clear and comprehensive results were gained. Consequently, only those places can be included in the investigation where the ground plan of the buildings has been established to such a degree that statements about the layout and types of building can be made.

Dan

The name Dan has survived in the form of an Arabic translation in the name *Tell el-Qāḍī*; the place is located on one of the sources of the Jordan. According to biblical tradition, the city was originally called Lajish and was only renamed after the settlement there of the tribe of Dan (cf. Josh. 19.47; Judg. 18.29). The Canaanite city is mentioned under this name in the execration texts, the documents from Mari and the list of Thutmosis III. During the period of the monarchy, Dan acquired a particular importance, because of its geographical position in the extreme north of the country and because of the building of a national shrine by Jeroboam I after the division of the kingdom in 926 (1 Kgs 12.28ff.). Its position near the border with the Aramaean state of Damascus led to its frequent destruction; the devastation brought under Benhadad I around 900 is mentioned in 1 Kgs 15.20; the city was finally destroyed during the Assyrian conquests under Tiglath-Pileser III (745–727).

The Iron Age city extends out over the area enclosed by the Canaanite city on the ruin-covered mound surrounded by the mighty fortifications of the Middle Bronze Age II (fig. 26).[1] As at Hazor, this was a new foundation, even though sporadic Early Iron Age settlements of minimal extent precede the new city. The strength of the fortifications, which were constructed towards the end of the tenth century, can be deduced from the mighty gate, located in the south at the foot of the mount. Originally built during the reign of Jeroboam I (926–907) as a four-chamber gate, it was further reinforced during the ninth century by a sort of preliminary gate with an entrance set at an angle. From the gate a paved path led upwards over the slope, through another gate and

---

1. A. Biran, 'Die Wiederentdeckung der alten Stadt Dan', *Antike Welt* 15/1 (1984), pp. 27-38; *idem*, 'Two Discoveries at Tel Dan', *IEJ* 30 (1980), pp. 89-98; *idem*, 'The Temenos at Dan', *Eretz Israel* 16 (1982), pp. 15-43 (in Hebrew); *idem*, 'The Dancer from Dan, the Empty Tomb and the Altar Room', *IEJ* 36 (1986), pp. 168-87.

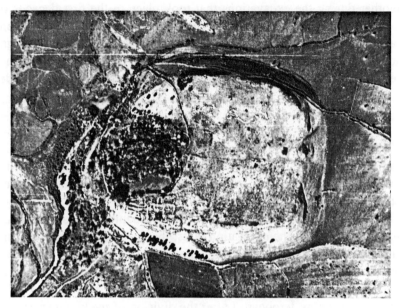

Figure 26. *Dan. Aerial photograph of the* tell.

into the centre of the city. It is probable that the lower gate was abandoned during the eighth century and only the upper gate on the edge of the plateau was rebuilt.

With the exception of a complex in the north-west of the city, nothing has yet been published about the building activity that had taken place inside the city. Information about the area which has been excavated has also not yet been adequately published, so that its significance is disputed and there is no sign as yet of a clear interpretation. A substructure built from carefully worked ashlar masonry with a free-standing stairway has been excavated, as have some outbuildings. In the opinion of A. Biran, the excavator, this platform, which measures 18.5 × 18.5 m, served as an open-air cultic place, which in contrast to a temple is termed a *bāmāh* in the biblical literature.[2] Although this interpretation is apparently supported by several cult objects which were found in the

---

2.   The term *bāmāh* need not be gone into in detail here; it denotes a place of sacrifice which is condemned as spurious under the Jerusalem temple theology. Up to the present the existence of such a place of sacrifice has not been demonstrated for the Iron Age. Cf. R. Amiran, 'The Tumuli West of Jerusalem', *IEJ* 8 (1958), pp. 206-27. For the term itself cf. P.H. Vaughan, *The Meaning of 'bāmâ' in the Old Testament* (1974).

vicinity of the platform, it does not stand up to critical examination.[3] Even though the structure has been robbed of material for building, the remains of partition walls and floors most likely call a habitable building to mind, and one which because of its size can be termed a palace. The building units discovered further to the west could certainly have been the adjacent buildings of a larger palace complex. Further publication of the findings must be awaited before a final categorization can be made. If the characterization of the structure as a palace were to prove correct, it should then be considered as the seat of a high-ranking official. Also there would not only have been an important cultic place in Dan, but the city would also have served as a centre of administration. Further details must be left open for the present, but the parts of the fortification and large buildings which have been excavated permit the recognition of careful city planning; how far the residential quarter was also included in the overall planning concept has not yet been revealed.

Hazor

During the Late Bronze Age, Hazor, with an area of 80 hectares (*c.* 200 acres), was the largest city ever built in the country in the pre-Hellenistic period. It comprised a small upper city built on remains of Early Bronze Age III and a lower city protected by a rampart, which extended northwards from it over a distance of about 1 km. The dominant position of the city is reflected in the various references made to it in the Akkadian and Egyptian sources; the name of one of the rulers, Abditirshi, is known from the Amarna letters (EA 227.228).[4] The story of the capture of Hazor by the Israelite tribes under the leadership of Joshua in Josh. 11.1–13 is of no value as a historical source, since it only arose at the end of the period of the monarchy and the incorporation of older traditions into it cannot be discerned.[5]

---

3. For the secular meaning of a single find cf. L.E. Stager and S.R. Wolff, 'Production and Commerce in Temple Courtyards: An Olive Press in the Sacred Precinct at Tel Dan', *BASOR* 243 (1981), pp. 95-102.

4. Yadin, *Hazor*, pp. 1-9 and 207.

5. Cf. V. Fritz, 'Das Ende der spätbronzezeitlichen Stadt Hazor Stratum XIII und die biblische Überlieferung in Josua 11 und Richter 4', *UF* 5 (1973), pp. 123-39. The list in Josh. 12 probably belongs to the period of Solomon and has nothing to do with the events at the end of the Late Bronze Age. Cf V. Fritz, 'Die sogenannte Liste der besiegten Könige in Josua 12', *ZDPV* 85 (1969), pp. 136-61.

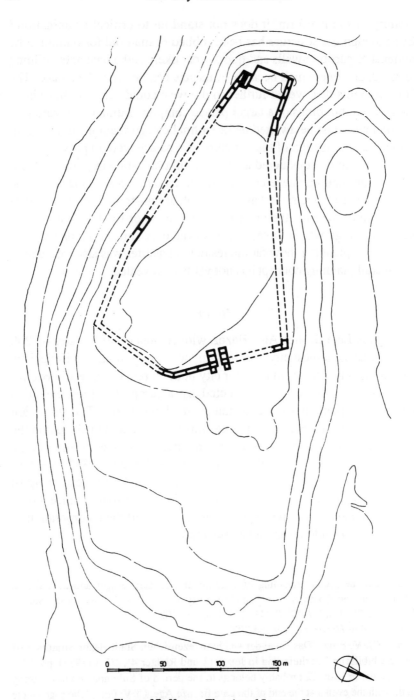

Figure 27. *Hazor. The city of Stratum X.*

After its destruction around 1200, Hazor remained a vast ruined site which today bears the name of *Tell Qedah*. The two small settlements of Stratum XII and Stratum XI only lasted for a short time in the twelfth and eleventh centuries and were extremely modest in size. It was Solomon who first rebuilt the city and fortified it as part of his measures to build up the kingdom, as is explicitly stated in 1 Kgs 9.15. This new foundation in Stratum X incorporated only the western half of the former upper city, as the excavations have shown; however, to date only small areas have been excavated (fig. 27).[6] The city was protected by a casemate wall, with a street running along its inner side, so that domestic buildings were separated from the fortifications. The individual rooms in the wall were accessible from this street. The city was entered on the eastern side via a mighty six-chamber gate with towers jutting out from the line of the city wall. At the western tip there was a small fort, which could not be examined more closely because the fortress-like building in Stratum VIII had been built on top of it; thus individual details are not known. Similarly nothing can be said at present about other public buildings which possibly existed there in addition to the private houses.

During the reign of Ahab (871–852) the city in Stratum VIII was probably enlarged to cover the whole area of the former upper city. At the same time as the alterations thus necessary were carried out, several new buildings were erected (fig. 28). This city differs so markedly in its layout, buildings and other structures from its predecessor, that it is possible to speak of a completely new ground plan.[7] A solid wall surrounded the previously open part of the plateau, but was connected in the north and south with the wall dating from the time of Solomon, which remained in use. Whether the additional extension on the eastern side was constructed during the same layer of occupation could not be definitely ascertained. It is possible that this small suburb, reached by a small postern on the northern side, was a further extension of the city from the period after Ahab. With the construction of the new wall on a different course, the wall in Stratum X which ran across the plateau went out of use, along with the gate. In the centre of the city there was a pillar-house with an annexe. A new fort was constructed at the western tip, which together with the adjacent buildings to the north and the south completed the fortifications at this point. The former casemate wall was filled in and thus transformed into a solid wall. Access to

6.   General plan in Yadin, *Hazor*, p. 111, Fig. 27; description pp. 135-46.
7.   Cf. Yadin, *Hazor*, pp. 165-78.

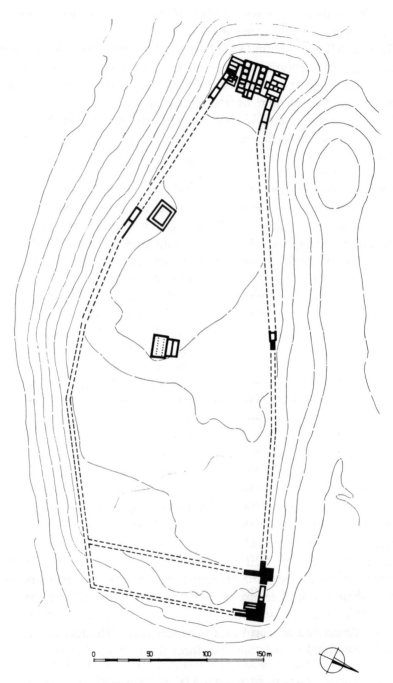

Figure 28. *Hazor. The city of Stratum VII.*

ground water was created by means of a shaft and tunnel construction
on the southern edge of the city, in order to secure the water supply in
times of siege (cf. below, Chapter 8). The position of the gate and details
of the network of streets are unknown. The parts of the built-up area
which have been excavated to date are not sufficient to allow a closer
characterization of the city to be made.

During the subsequent course of the history of the settlement (Strata
VII–V) new building took place on the site of the pillar-house and the
western tip was reinforced by the construction of a new wall. The
domestic architecture of the later occupation levels allows recognition of
a certain social differentiation.[8] Although the transition from one occupation level to another brought changes, the city was able to carry on
within its established framework until its final destruction in Stratum V A
by Tiglath-Pileser III in 734 (cf. 2 Kgs 15.29). After the Assyrian
conquest only isolated houses within the city precinct have been built. A
palace with a large inside courtyard was constructed in Stratum III on
the site of the former fort; this served as the seat of an Assyrian city
governor who administered the province or at least a certain part of it.[9]

Kinneret

During the period of the monarchy, Kinneret was the most important
city on Lake Gennesaret, which bore its name in the pre-Hellenistic
period. The town was already mentioned in the list of Tuthmosis III
together with other cities in the upper Jordan valley, but in the Bible it
only occurs in Josh. 19.35 as belonging to the tribe of Naphtali. Its
identification with *Tell el-'Oreime* by G. Dalman and W.F. Albright is
unquestionable; the area taken up by the habitation is not only confined
to the small tell on the summit, but also includes the whole of the slope
which descends to the lake.[10] Since different areas of the slope were
built upon in different periods, the result was not the creation of a
mound of ruins, but rather an overlapping of the individual occupation
layers. Only in Early Bronze Age II does the city seem to have
embraced the whole of the slope within a surrounding wall, while the

8.   Cf. the plans of Strata VI and V of Sector A in Yadin, *Hazor*, p. 180, Figs.
48 and 186, Fig. 50.

9.   Cf. G. Dalman, *Orte und Wege Jesu* (2nd edn, 1921), pp. 118-20.

10.   V. Fritz, 'Kinneret: Excavations at Tell el-'Oreimeh (Tel Kinrot) 1982–1985
Seasons', *Tel Aviv* 20 (1993), pp. 187-215.

Canaanite city probably only extended over the lower part of the slope.[11] Only very scant remains of both cities could be excavated to date.

An open village dating to the eleventh century precedes the foundation of the Iron Age city but its remains are only sparsely preserved. As the pottery shows, the new city in Stratum V was built at the time of the reign of David and is thus older than Hazor, which was built under Solomon. The city wall, which was encountered in three locations, had a width of between 6 and 11 m, thus exceeding that of all the other solid walls of Iron Age II. The wall was especially protected by means of a supporting wall running at an oblique angle out in front. The fortifications probably enclosed the whole slope and with it an area of 5 hectares (*c.* 12.5 acres), although their complete course could not be ascertained. Of the building which had been carried on there, only a palace situated half way up the hill has been partly excavated to date; this probably stood at the centre. More public buildings were detected near the city wall in the north-east and south-west, whilst domestic houses have not yet come to light.

Before the construction of the various buildings the ground was terraced by the deposition of material. This constructional measure and the extraordinarily strong fortifications point to a special planning concept for the city, even though closer details have not yet been established. The existence of a large number of buildings of an official character permits the assumption that they served a particular function where administrative business was concerned. This city of the early period of the monarchy did not long survive the division of the kingdom in 926, but the absence of a destruction level indicates that it was abandoned by the inhabitants, albeit for reasons unknown. During the ninth century only a modest watchtower stood on the site of the city (Stratum III).

Because of the long interruption in the history of the settlement, there is no line of continuity between the newly-built city in Stratum II— which dates to around 800—and the city of the tenth century; thus it also exhibits a completely new plan in all details (fig. 29). Since only the summit of the hill was now fortified, the area of the city was confined to 1 hectare (*c.* 2.5 acres), but individual houses also seem to have been located outside the protecting wall. The nature of the fortification is unique in ancient Israel, in that it boasts a total of four towers on the north-east and north-west sides which are not incorporated into the wall

11. Cf. S.M.M. Winn and J. Yakar, 'The 1982 Excavations at Tel Kinrot: The Early Bronze Age Settlement', *Tel Aviv* 11 (1984), pp. 20-47.

in the usual way, but represent independent elements within the fortification. Two of them have been completely excavated and measure about 11 × 11 and 22 × 23 m respectively; the existence of the other two towers is indicated by the presence of great piles of stones on the line followed by the wall. These bastion-like towers were probably inhabited in their upper part, but no remains of their internal construction have been found.[12] There were inward and outward jutting sections in the lengths of wall between the towers, with the width of the wall varying between 4 and 2.8 m. It is notable that towers are absent on the south-west and south-east sides. The gate in the south-east was constructed as a simple two-chambered gate; although only the south-west half of it has been excavated to date, its typological characterization is certain.

Inside the city next to the gate there was a row of pillar-houses, set parallel to the city wall. Although only one unit has been excavated, the existence of two other buildings of this kind is conjectured, forming a continuation in a north-westerly direction. As an official function is to be assumed for this type of building, their location points to preliminary planning. There was a private house built in Israelite tradition on the north-western side. This was separated from the wall by a street, but the open space was extensively built upon in a second phase of building; at the same time, the house was enlarged through the addition of outbuildings. Another private house, which can be conjectured as a four-room house, was situated in the north-eastern area. It can be seen from these two houses that a row of houses probably extended along the city wall and was parallel to it. The streets ran past the houses. The building that took place here corresponds to that of the ancient Israelite residential city, and the complex of pillar-houses indicates that administrative duties were carried out there. The regular pattern of streets stems from careful planning.

After its destruction in the course of the Assyrian conquests under Tiglath-Pileser III in 734, the city in Stratum II was not rebuilt. However, a settlement was established once more amidst the ruins of the mighty fortifications during the last decades of the eighth century, although this can no longer be described as a city (Stratum I). The south-western area was fortified anew by means of a connecting wall, with the

12. Demonstrated in U. Hübner, 'Wohntürme im eisenzeitlichen Israel?', *BN* 41 (1988), pp. 23-30.

The City in Ancient Israel

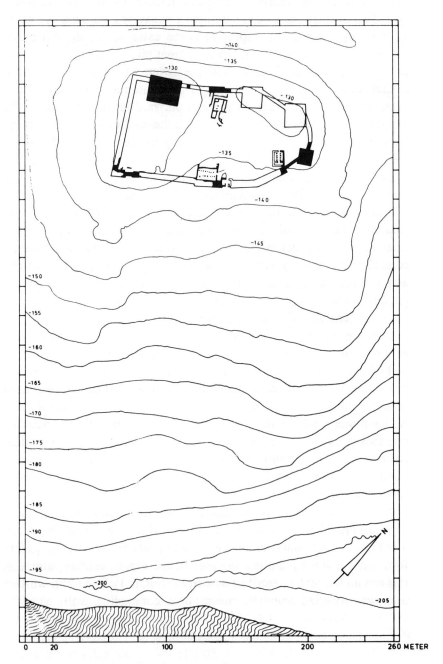

Figure 29. *Kinneret. The city of Stratum II.*

incorporation of the large tower. A passageway which could be closed was left open for access, but there was no attempt to build it out into a gate structure. There are notable variations in the types of building that was carried on inside the fortified area. A carefully constructed four-room house stood to the north-east of the entrance, abutting the inner side of the tower, and next to it there was an outbuilding subdivided by a row of pillars, with a water storage cistern in front of it. By contrast in the southern corner there was a small group of buildings, consisting of one- and two-room houses in simple rows next to each other, with walls measuring only the width of one stone. A further residential unit abutted the north-eastern tower and was surrounded by a simple wall. This settlement constitutes but a poor sequel to the former city, in which the fortifications were re-used and the old forms of building sometimes employed. The impression of the settlement as a whole is one of weakness and poverty; it probably failed to survive the further campaigns conducted by the Assyrians at the time of Sennacherib before and after 700. A palace in Assyrian style was built on the slope during the seventh century, its purpose being to administer the area. This marks the end of urban development at Kinneret.

Megiddo

The Canaanite city as it existed during the Late Bronze Age perished around 1150 in Stratum VII A (cf. above, Chapter 3). Although the subsequent settlement in Strata VI B and VI A no longer follow in the urban tradition, they still differ radically from the newly-founded settlements of the Israelite tribes in the prestate period (cf. above, Chapter 4). When both these possibilities are considered, its likeliest characterization is that of a settlement in continuation of the former city culture; the palace west of the gate was even restored in Stratum VI A but the temple was not rebuilt (fig. 8). Thus Stratum V B constitutes a new village, but because of the bad state of preservation a closer understanding of it is not possible. By contrast the settlement in Stratum V A presents a defensive aspect once again (fig. 30); despite the absence of a city wall, this occupation level still exhibits various elements of an urban nature. As the new order is to be traced back to the planning concepts of a central authority, Stratum V A exhibits details of Israelite urbanization. It is the occupation level in Stratum IV B that can first be understood as an Israelite city in the true sense (fig. 31); city wall, gate complex and various public buildings give it a clear urban character.

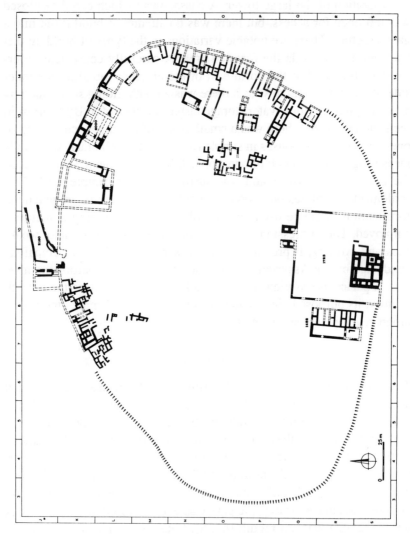

Figure 30. *Megiddo. The settlement of Stratum V A.*

After a second phase of this city in Stratum IV A, which for the most part can be distinguished by the conversion of the city gate into a four-chambered gate, Stratum III represents a new foundation with a complete renewal of the city plan (fig. 32).

Numerous details of the stratigraphical progression are just as controversial in nature as the relative dating of the occupation levels.[13]

13. A. Kempinski, *Megiddo. A City-State and Royal Centre in North Israel*

Since a solution can only be found to the controversial questions when all the excavation results and the material have been studied, the reconstruction of Strata V A, IV B and III by Z. Herzog will be used as a basis here, since it has brought together those areas of buildings that belong together with a certain logical consistency.[14] Decisive is an understanding that palace 1723 and the six-chamber gate incorporated into the solid wall must have belonged to different occupation levels. Despite the solution to the stratigraphical problem, difficulties remain where the dating is concerned, with the particular question as to which level is to be identified with the city of Solomon, as mentioned in 1 Kgs 9.15. If, in accordance with D. Ussishkin, the notion that the six-chamber gate must be associated with the building activities of Solomon[15] is discarded, then the following absolute chronology is arrived at, in agreement with the pottery:[16]

Stratum VI A	second half of the eleventh century
Stratum V B	first half of the tenth century
Stratum V A	second half of the tenth century
Stratum IV B	first half of the ninth century
Stratum IV A	second half of the ninth century and first half of the eighth century
Stratum III	After 733 and the seventh century

Accordingly, Stratum V A is to be seen as the new foundation by Solomon, which replaced a modest village of the time of David. The decisive building phase in Stratum IV B thus belongs to the period after

(1989), pp. 78-103; Y. Yadin, 'New Light on Solomon's Megiddo', *BA* 23 (1960), pp. 62-68; K.M. Kenyon, *Megiddo, Hazor, Samaria and Chronology* (University of London Institute of Archaeology, Bulletin 4; 1964); Y. Aharoni, 'The Stratification of Israelite Megiddo', *JNES* 31 (1972), pp. 302-11; Y. Yadin, 'Megiddo of the Kings of Israel', *BA* 33 (1970), pp. 66-96; Y. Shiloh, 'Solomon's City Gate at Megiddo as recorded by its excavator, R. Lamon, Chicago', *Levant* 12 (1980), pp. 69-76.

14. Z. Herzog, in *Architecture*, pp. 212-17. The system of the numbering of the strata applied there is also followed here, as a clear division is made between Stratum VA and Stratum IVB. Cf. the version already given by Z. Herzog, *Das Stadtor in Israel und in den Nachbarländern* (1986), pp. 93-108.

15. D. Ussishkin, 'Was the "Solomonic" City Gate at Megiddo Built by King Solomon?', *BASOR* 239 (1980), pp. 1-18, contra Y. Yadin 'Solomon's City Wall and Gate at Gezer', *IEJ* 8 (1958), pp. 80-86; cf also Y. Yadin, 'A Rejoinder', *BASOR* 239 (1980), pp. 19-23.

16. Cf. the more recent examination by G.J. Wightman, 'Megiddo VI A-III: Associated Structure and Chronology', *Levant* 17 (1985), pp. 117-29.

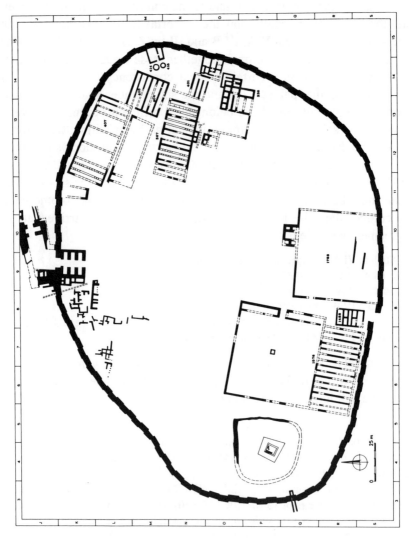

Figure 31. *Megiddo. The city of Stratum IV B.*

the division of the kingdom, which took place at the end of the rule of
Solomon in 926. The transition between the two Stratums of settlement
took place after Megiddo was captured by the Pharaoh Sheshonk,
whose campaign in 922 is documented by the fragment of a stele bearing his name from Megiddo.[17]

17. Cf. K.A. Kitchen, *The Third Intermediate Period in Egypt (1100–650)*
(1973), pp. 294-300 and 432-47.

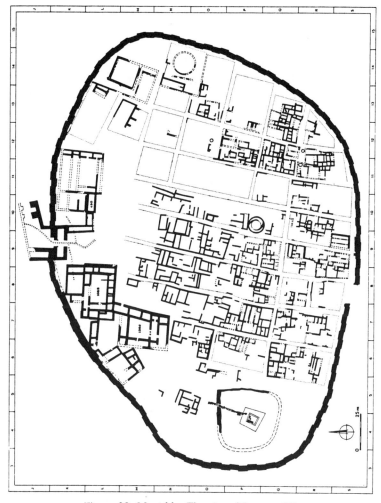

Figure 32. *Megiddo. The city of Stratum III.*

In the village of Stratum V A, a new foundation around 950, the position of the gate is retained. This is a two-chamber gate, of which only the western half has survived. (The foremost pier of the gate is missing in the plan in fig. 30, but the remains of it are shown in the final publication).[18] There is no city wall, the fortification consisting rather of the external walls of the buildings on the edge of the city, where the houses are positioned next to each other without gaps between them. This

---

18. G. Loud, *Megiddo II. Seasons of 1935-39. Text* (1948), Fig. 388.

defensive arrangement is only partly recognizable because the outer
edge is covered by the city wall of Stratum IV B which was built upon
it, and partly destroyed by the deep foundations of the latter. Because of
their bad state of preservation, no categorization of the houses as to type
is possible. The variant type of the four-room house with one further
room in front is found on the eastern edge. The employment of prestate
forms of building cannot be deduced from the remaining houses.

Palace 1723 was situated on the southern edge of the city, inside an
open area surrounded by a wall and accessible from the north via a gate
with four chambers. It was almost square in form, measuring 23×21.5 m,
and built of carefully hewn stones, some of which bore masons' marks.
The foundations reached a depth of about 1.5 m but nothing has been
preserved from the upper parts of the walls except for the last course
above the floor; thus the method of access to the individual rooms and
the concept behind the building cannot be definitely ascertained. The
rooms were apparently arranged around a central court, surrounding it
on all sides. The entrance was probably in the east, as is indicated by the
position of a stairwell and a platform paved with stones in front of the
building. The layout of Palace 1723 owes much to the courtyard type of
house and thus follows Canaanite building tradition;[19] it could have been
the seat of a city governor. There was a relationship between the palace
and building 1482 on the eastern side, as can be adduced from its position and orientation. It comprises a total of four units, identical in their
form, and two large courtyards at the back. The individual elements
each consist of a courtyard and two rooms on one of the long sides. It
may have been occupied by officials in connection with the city
administration.

Because of its incomplete plan, building 6000 on the northern edge
cannot be definitely categorized. On the evidence of the parts which
have been excavated to date, this was a building in which the rooms
were grouped with great regularity around an open court, once again
reflecting Canaanite building tradition. In this sector, the fortifications
exhibit the character of a casemate wall. Building 6000, which is situated
to the west of the 'palace' also seems to have had a public function, but

19. The interpretation as a Hilani in D. Ussishkin, 'King Solomon's Palace and
Building 1723 in Megiddo', *IEJ* 16 (1966), pp. 174-86, fails to recognize the character
of the layout of the building, cf. by contrast V. Fritz, *Die syrische Bauform des Hilani
und die Frage seiner Verbreitung* (Damaszener Mitteilungen 1; 1983), pp. 43-58.

its ground plan cannot be reconstructed from the remains that have been uncovered.

In contrast to the ordered layout of the palace precinct, the rest of the city only shows minimal signs of planning. In order to achieve the desired defensive aspect, the houses on the periphery formed an unbroken row; thus the city could only be entered via the gate. The pattern of streets cannot be discerned, and a particular set of planning precepts does not seem to have been followed. Only palace 1723 gives the city a special character, and possibly a straight way ran from the gate to its entrance. In size, layout and method of building this palace stands in stark contrast to the other buildings. The building up of the city and its enlargement by Solomon, as mentioned in 1 Kgs 9.15, are to be assigned to Stratum V, which in addition to the residential quarters also included buildings for officials appointed by the king. It was the responsibility of these officials to carry out the administration under the kingship. However, when compared with the royal building measures in the city of the ninth century, the number of buildings with an official function was minimal; thus its character as a residential city was not altered significantly.

After the capture of Megiddo by Shoshenk in 922 the city in Stratum IV B was completely rebuilt (fig. 31). This was not brought about by necessity, since Megiddo was probably not destroyed by Shoshenk; it was, instead, a royal measure implemented to provide the location with the buildings necessary for its new role and to fortify it accordingly. Both the buildings within the city and the fortifications are reflections of a planning and design which were necessary to achieve an objective—the deployment of state authority.

The gate remained in its old location, but was redesigned as a six-chamber gate with a preliminary gate on an ascending path and built of hewn stone. The inner gate construction had a primarily civil function. The solid wall, 4 m thick, had outward and inward projecting sections at regular intervals. Only little is preserved of the residential buildings to the west and south-west of the gate. The largest area was taken up by two complexes containing pillar-houses, which were situated in the south and north-east of the city. The southern complex 1576 consisted of a total of five units 28 m long, with an open area 55 m square in front of them. On the eastern side of this square there were two other rooms with the entranceway leading through between them. A type of basin made of mud-brick was situated in the middle. The walled square of the former palace 1723 to the east of this building remained in use after the building itself had been removed down to the foundation walls; the loss of the former entrance meant that the new one had to be sought on the western side. Between the two there is unit 1482, reduced in size, and now only consisting of two courtyards each with two rooms adjoining them.

The area of buildings in the north-east consisted of three complexes of pillar-houses (407, 403/4 and 367), which stood almost at right angles to one other. That to the east only comprised two units, whereas the other two both contained five units, each measuring about 25 m in length. In the area surrounded by these complexes stood a building which can only be approximately reconstructed.[20] It exhibits a precise organization of the rooms around an open courtyard and appears in all probability to have been used in close connection with the pillar-houses. It is an undisputed fact that the pillar-houses were put to official or public use,[21] in connection with administrative or military duties of the kingdom. Since almost the complete repertoire of ceramics was brought to light amongst the finds there, this type of building would hardly have served as a stable for the horses or as a storehouse. As all other interpretations also fail to hold up, given the structural details of the building, it can be taken as a certainty that the pillar-houses, standing in a row, were used as barracks to house troops.[22] Thus Megiddo Stratum IV B is most likely described as a garrison city.

A palace, building 338, lay to the south-east of this complex of pillar-houses, with a large courtyard in front and further buildings bordering onto it; of these building 401 probably served as a storeroom. The whole area was separated off by a wall and was only accessible via a gate which resembled that in the encircling wall of palace 1723 in Stratum V A. There was, however, a connecting way leading in a northwards

20. Cf. here G.J. Wightman, 'Building 434 and Other Public Buildings in the Northeastern Sector of Megiddo', *Tel Aviv* 11 (1984), pp. 132-45.

21. The controversy over the interpretation of the pillar-houses built in rows was fuelled by the complexes found at Megiddo. Cf. J. Pritchard, 'The Megiddo Stables: A Reassessment', in *Archaeology in the Twentieth Century*, pp. 268-76.

22. Cf. V. Fritz, 'Bestimmung und Herkunft des Pfeilerhauses in Israel', *ZDPV* 93 (1977), pp. 30-45.

direction between this place and the area containing the complexes of pillar-houses. Palace 338 can therefore be considered as the seat of the commanding officer.

A shaft was constructed in the south-western area of the city from which a tunnel could be reached that led to the water source situated outside the city wall. The area around the shaft was protected by a surrounding wall. The water source was concealed by deposited material so that it was no longer visible on the ground. By this means the water source was accessible from inside the city and the water supply secured, even in times of siege (cf. Chapter 8).

Thus the kings of Israel built up Megiddo into a well-fortified and, for a certain period, self-sufficient troop base in case of siege. The accommodation for the members of the army and the open areas associated with it take up wide areas of the city. Commensurate with its military importance, the private houses only filled a 'quarter' in the north-west of the city. The function of the city as the base for troops clearly conditioned its layout. The king, as supreme commander-in-chief, ordered the building measures whose concept and execution allow recognition of a high level of planning and organization.

Megiddo existed on into Stratum IV A during the eighth century without any great changes. However, the city gate was reduced to four chambers. The Israelite city was finally conquered and destroyed by Tiglath-Pileser III in 734.

With the transformation of state territory into the provinces Gilead, Megiddo and Dor by the Assyrians, Megiddo became a provincial capital. The new political importance connected with the latter status is reflected in Stratum III (fig. 32), which dates from after 734 and lasted roughly until the eclipse of Assyrian supremacy around 630. Streets running from north to south in an almost straight line divide the city into individual blocks of about 20 m in width. A complete subdivision into *insulae* was not achieved, however, since the streets running from east to west do not follow a complete, unbroken course. Nevertheless, the resulting pattern is unknown for the Israelite period of the monarchy and is due to foreign influence. The network of streets was clearly established before the houses were built; its course is orientated towards the gate. This organizational principle for the layout of a city is widely met in the Mesopotamian area during the second and first millenia and would have been introduced by the Assyrians into their provincial capital.[23]

The gate is a simple two-chamber construction of notable size, and the city wall and shaft leading to the water source continued in use. Two palaces in the style of Mesopotamian courtyard houses, which were later linked to each other, were constructed to the west of the gate. Only in the case of palace 1369 are the audience rooms on the southern side, following usual practice, while palace 1052 was constructed on an east-west orientation. There are other buildings in their vicinity, and the whole complex was the seat of the Assyrian governor. The large building to the east of the gate cannot be more closely categorized, but it probably served an administrative purpose. The house types are extremely varied and the large number of almost square courtyards with which the houses were provided is notable. Apart from the courtyard type of house there are also units which consist of long rooms situated alongside each other. Two large circular silos, of which one is set into the ground, point to a centrally administered system for the storage of provisions.

As administrative headquarters of the province, Megiddo Stratum III is really a residential city, in which only the palace and the large building next to the gate indicate its particular status. After the collapse of Assyrian domination the city plan was largely retained during Stratum II, until the city was finally destroyed after the battle lost by Josiah against the Pharaoh Necho in 609 (cf. 2 Kgs 23.29).

Tell el-Fār'ah

Because of the rich water source of *'En Fār'ah* about 200 metres to the north-east there were already fortified cities on *Tell el-Fār'ah* in Early Bronze Age II and Middle Bronze Age II B. The location was only sporadically settled during the Late Bronze Age, and the minimal remains found there exclude the existence of a city. The new occupation during Iron Age I in Stratum VII took the form of an open village with building forms typical of the period; the houses, which have walls only one stone in width, are badly preserved.[24] The area built upon clearly extends over and beyond the Middle Bronze Age city wall. Without doubt, this occupation level represents one of the newly-founded villages of the eleventh century.

23. Cf. by way of an example the plans of the cities of Saduppum and Babylon by E. Heinrich in W. Orthmann, *Der alte Orient* (1975), Figs. 56 and 81.
24. A. Chambon, *Tell el-Far'ah I. L'âge du fer* (1984), Plan II.

Where Iron Age II is concerned, three occupation levels can be differentiated. These can be dated as follows:

Stratum VII b	tenth century
Stratum VII d	eighth/ninth centuries
Stratum VII e	seventh century

Stratum VII e only represents a reuse of Stratum VII d and can thus be disregarded here. In the case of Stratum VII c, which only comprises one single building, Helga Weippert has demonstrated convincingly that it represents a second building phase of Stratum VII d, which can be dated to the second half of the eighth century.[25] The assertion of the excavator R. de Vaux that the Middle Bronze Age fortifications were reused in Iron Age II presents great difficulties where the reconstruction of the ground plan is concerned.[26] Against his theory stands the fact that both in Stratum VII b and in Stratum VII d house walls extend out over the former city wall and the reuse of the gate is by no means certain.[27] Thus for the time being, the question of whether and in what way the place was fortified during Iron Age II remains open. The absence of a single profile or section and numerous inadequacies in the plans make a clear decision impossible; thus the question of the fortifications cannot be resolved at present. The results that can be verified make the theory put forward by the excavator rather improbable, since there was no city wall at all in Iron Age II. For this reason the former equation of the mound with Tirza is questionable, since an unfortified location can hardly have served as the temporary capital of the kings of Israel (cf. 1 Kgs 14.17; 15.21-33; 16.6ff.).[28] Leaving aside the necessity of a new attempt to establish the identity of *Tell el-Fār'ah*, the quarter which has been uncovered on the western edge of the mound should briefly be discussed here in view of its peculiar nature.

Stratum VII b is hardly to be differentiated from the preceding Stratum VII a, although it is considerably better preserved (fig. 33). For the most part, it consists of four-room houses of varying types (442, 440, 161, 410 A, 436, 355, 384). These are set in irregular rows of

25 H. Weippert, *ZDPV* 101 (1985), pp. 178-83.

26. R. de Vaux, 'Tirzah', in D.W. Thomas (ed.), *Archaeology and Old Testament Study* (1967), pp. 371-83.

27. Chambon, *Tell el-Far'ah I. L'âge du fer*, Plans III and V.

28. The positive view of U. Jochims in 'Thirza und die Ausgrabungen auf dem *Tell el-fār'a'*, *ZDPV* 76 (1960), pp. 73-96, is still fully influenced by the excavator's own views.

varying orientation. Areas in front of or next to the individual houses could be used as additional outside courtyards (163). The method of building is extremely insubstantial, since the walls are mostly of only one stone's width. The average house covers an area of about 100 sq m. The pattern of streets is irregular, and only in exceptional instances do several houses form a smooth façade together. The almost north-south orientation is maintained throughout the whole quarter so that practically all the streets cross at right angles.

A fundamental change occurred in Stratum VII d (fig. 34). Although simple four-room houses (362, 366, 336) are still to be found in the southern part of the site, the larger part is taken over by new buildings, whose size and method of construction differentiate them substantially from 'normal houses' (148, 327, 328). Here, in spite of enlargement by means of additional courtyards and annexes, the desire to construct the nucleus of the house according to the form of the four-room house is clear, even if the use of stone pillars has largely been abandoned. This tendency to enlarge the house without changing the basic ground plan is above all recognizable in the case of house 148. A paved courtyard 10 m in square was set in front of the actual four-room house 148 with its side rooms and room at the back. More rooms had been added on the western side. By contrast the rooms adjacent on the eastern side did not necessarily belong to this complex, since the location of the entrances could only be hypothetically suggested but not proved. (The same method of enlargement can be seen in house 411 from a later building phase in this occupation layer). House 328 also seems to have had a courtyard in front of it, in the form of Locus 353 A. The objective of providing the houses with outside courtyards, already recognizable in Stratum VII b, has been systematically incorporated into the ground plan of the houses in Stratum VII d. The enlargement of the ground area to 120 or 150 sq m and the improved method of building indicate that a better economic position was enjoyed by the inhabitants. Despite the straight alignment of the walls there was no prior planning; other indications of conceptual city planning are also absent. In spite of the considerable improvement in building, the place remained an agricultural settlement.

The equation of Mizpa with *Tell en-Naṣbe* about 13 km to the north of Jerusalem can be confirmed as a result of topographical considerations.[29]

29. H. Donner, 'Der Feind aus dem Norden', *ZDPV* 84 (1968), pp. 46-54.

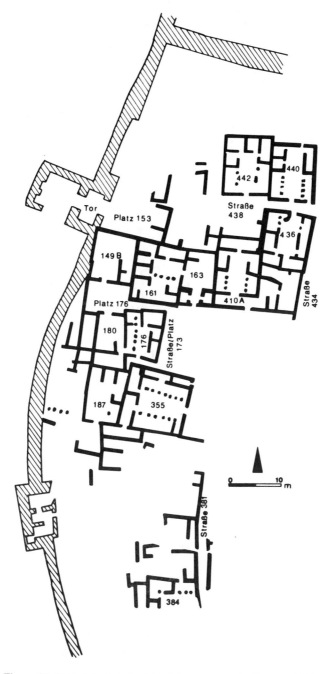

Figure 33. Tell el-Fār'a *(North). Living quarters in Stratum VII b.*

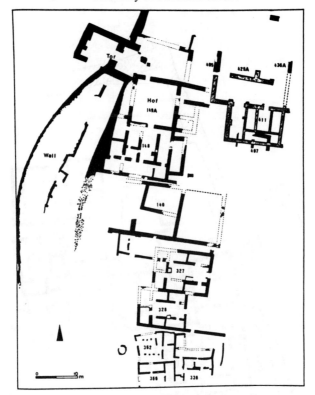

Figure 34. Tell el-Fār'a *(North). Living quarters in Stratum VII d.*

Mizpa

Since the occupation layers were not carefully differentiated and sepa-rated during the excavations, the ground plan of the city in the individ-ual periods cannot be ascertained, although large expanses of the city were uncovered. On the basis of subsequent analysis, four occupation levels can be distinguished:

Phase A — an unfortified village
Phase B — a city with casemate wall, towers and two-chambered gate
Phase C — a city with solid wall, towers and two-chambered gate
Phase D — a reuse of phase C

A chronological determination on the basis of pottery has thus not yet been achieved; the sources indicate that occupation can already be reck-oned with here in the prestate period (Judg. 20, 21; 1 Sam. 7.5ff.; 10.17). Where the period of the monarchy is concerned, enlargement of the settlement by Asa (908–868) into a Judaean fortress is emphatically mentioned (1 Kgs 15.22). After the destruction of Jerusalem by Nebuchadnezzar in 587, this location was the seat of Gedalja, whom the Babylonians appointed governor and who was later murdered there (2 Kgs 25.23; Jer. 40.7ff., 41). If phase D came to an end shortly after 587 it probably existed during the seventh century, then the city of phase C can be dated to the ninth/eighth century, the preceding phase B is thus to be placed in the tenth century, and phase A belongs to the eleventh century.

The city of phase B (fig. 35) is thus preceded by a prestate settlement, of which no details are available. Parts of a solid wall from the fortifications in phase B are preserved, with private houses built directly onto them.[30] These houses follow the Israelite building form of the four- and three-room house with its variants. The positioning and arrangement of the units do not follow any recognizable scheme, the pattern of streets is highly irregular and a street running in the form of a ring parallel to the city wall is absent. Signs of city planning are not evident and the houses form an extremely dense agglomeration without alignment or organization. Public buildings were not discovered, since a larger part of the area covered by the city had been destroyed by erosion. During phase B, Mizpa was a residential city without conspicuous social differentiation among its inhabitants.

In phase C, the city was enclosed within a new wall (fig. 35), which had an average width of 4 m; sections of it jutted both outwards and inwards, and it had numerous towers. The extraordinarily strong fortifications were constructed outside the former ring of walls and give the city a fortress-like character. Its function as a Judaean border fort against the northern kingdom of Israel is thus reflected in its imposing fortifications. It is to be assumed here that the older city wall was removed, together with its towers, and used as building material for the new wall. The domestic buildings correspond broadly to those in phase B, but large four-room houses were built in the newly-acquired area between the old and new city wall. With a ground area of 120 sq m or more, these differed in size to the older private houses. It is possible that these houses were provided for Judaeans who held special office or function in the city.[31] More new buildings were found in the area of the

30. The views on the layout of the city differ from that of T.L. McClellan, 'Town Planning at *Tell en-Naṣbeh*', *ZDPV* 100 (1984), pp. 53-69.

31. Cf. K. Branigan, 'The Four Room Building of Tell en-Naṣbeh', *IEJ* 16 (1966), pp. 206-208.

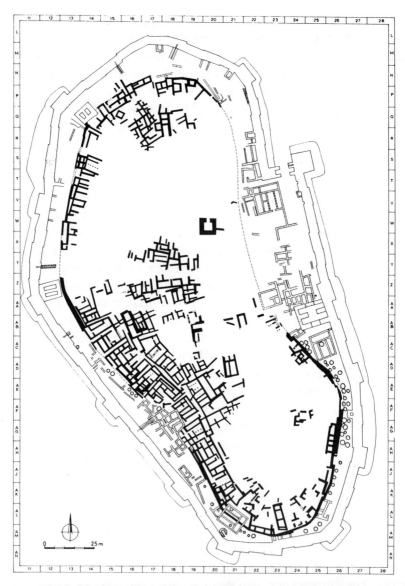

Figure 35. *Mizpa. The city in phase B (black) and phase C (white).*

disused city gate. Even with these changes in the nature of the building, Mizpa remained a residential city, since it cannot be proved that troops were stationed there. Even after its transfer to Judah and the construction of stronger fortifications Mizpa still belongs among the simple provincial cities and there are no peculiarities in the building that went on there.

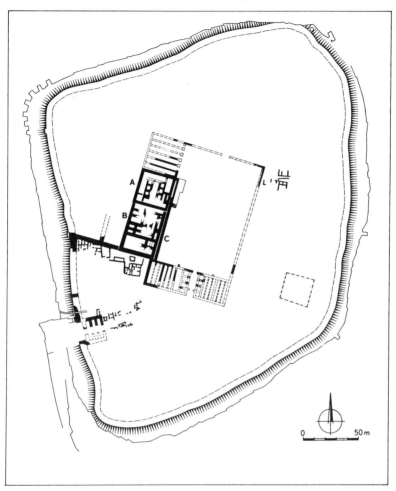

Figure 36. *Lachish. Palace and city of Stratum III.*

Lachish

Doubts about the location of Lachish on *Tell ed-Duwēr* in the Shefela have never been silenced, but they can be regarded as unjustified on the grounds of the excavation results. The *tell* is an imposing mound, which was formed from the settlement layers of Early Bronze Age I–III, Middle Bronze Age II B and the Late Bronze Age, but it is relatively small covering an area of only 1.5 hectares. The place remained uninhabited for a time after the final destruction of the last Canaanite city, and the new foundation of a settlement only took place there during the course of the tenth century (Stratum V). There was a decisive phase of further building in the ninth century, when it was not only strongly fortified but a palace was also added (fig. 36). The building activity lasted until the conquest by Sennacherib in 701 (Strata IV and III). A resumption of settlement then took place in the second half of the seventh century but this only constituted a pale reflection of what had been there before (Stratum II).[32]

The fortifications consisted of a double ring of walls, in which the space between the two walls was devoid of any buildings. The lower wall had projecting as well as recessed sections and supporting walls, but there were no towers. The upper wall is between 5 and 6 m in width. No tower has yet been discovered, but it can be assumed that there were once towers here. The only gate was on the west side, and consisted of an ascending path, a bastion-like projecting gate construction and a six-chamber gate, which extended inside the city.

The centre of the city was dominated by a palace complex, which occupied about one-sixth of the total area. This included a large residential building, a row of six storerooms, an entrance building and an open square. The main building stood on a platform, the walls of which are still extant to a height of 7 m. The northern and southern halves were built consecutively in two construction phases, but belong together chronologically. The platform had been filled in with debris material and thus formed a substructure for the building. Little remains of the rooms were preserved, because the so-called 'residency' in Stratum I was built over them. Thus the ground plan of the building will remain incomplete. Perhaps the division of the platform into two parts of 32 × 32 m and 45 × 32 m in size represented a subdivision of the building into two constructional units of differing size. The division into rooms is no longer completely discernible but the rooms were possibly arranged around a court. The entrance was on the eastern side, via an open stairway from the large square.

A row of 6 long rooms was added north of the building, and clearly served the purpose of storage. In the south, an entrance complex had been constructed in front of the square in the east of the palace. This consists of a gate construction with six chambers and two other rooms in the 'towers', as well as a total of four units, each of which were subdivided by small partition walls into three elongated halls. The courtyard,

32. D. Ussishkin, 'Excavations at Tel Lachish 1973–77, Preliminary Report', *Tel Aviv* 5 (1978), pp. 1-97 and *idem*, 'Excavation at Tel Lachish 1978–1983, Second Preliminary Report', *Tel Aviv* 10 (1983), pp. 97-175.

which extended over the total length of the palace at the eastern side, was surrounded by a wall, as can be deduced from exposed sections. No explanation can be found for the purpose of the cross-wall which continues on the course of the south wall and connects with the city wall. A street leads from the city gate to the entrance gate of the palace complex. Up to the present, no parts of the residential buildings worthy of mention have been excavated.

The unique palace at Lachish combines three different buildings which are grouped on two sides around a large courtyard, and serve different functions. The residential building was the seat of the city governor, to whom the king had entrusted the administration of the province. The storage magazines indicate the practice of intermediate storage of dues paid in actual goods and products, or of the yield obtained from land which was crown property. Servants and staff were housed in the southern tract, with its four units of pillar-houses. Parallels for this closed complex have not been found to date. Only palace 1723 in Megiddo, dating to the tenth century, was situated on the edge of an open courtyard (cf. fig. 30); the large outside court thus seems to have been a typical feature of palace complexes. Thus the administrative and military functions of the city governor who resided here cannot be divorced from one another as far as the allocation of duties is concerned, since both were probably carried out by the same person. The numerous stamps on the handles of jars point to a well-organized administration, but details are not known.[33] Although the storage jars bearing these stamps are connected with the necessary provisioning of the army or of officials appointed by the king, it cannot as yet be ascertained whether the respective contents originated from levies or from royal reserves. At any rate these stamps, which mention the names of four cities—Hebron, Socho, Sif and *Mmst*—point to the fact that Judah was a highly structured state, due to the centralized control exercised by the monarchy in economic and military spheres. Thus Lachish was a centre of royal administration.

Biblical tradition does not provide any information about the particular role of Lachish, although it was mentioned more often than other

33. Cf. the various solutions offered by P. Welten, *Die Königs-Stempel. Ein Beitrag zur Militärpolitik Judas unter Hiskia und Josua* (1969); D. Ussishkin, 'Royal Judean Storage Jars and Private Seal Impressions', *BASOR* 223 (1976), pp. 1-13; Aharoni, *The Land of the Bible*, pp. 394-400.

cities during the period of the monarchy.[34] According to Josh. 15.29
Lachish belonged to the third district of the provinces of Judah, but the
dating of this document in the ninth century is disputed. However, the
precedence of the city is clear from the note in 2 Kgs 14.19 = 2 Chron.
25.27, according to which Amaziah (801–773) fled in the face of an
uprising from Jerusalem to Lachish, and was killed there.

During his campaign in 701 Sennacherib sent an embassy to Jerusalem
from Lachish, after the conquest of a number of cities in the Shefela. By
the time it had returned, however, the Assyrian king had already moved
on to Libna, since his troops had captured Lachish in the meantime
(2 Kgs 18.4; 19.8 = 2 Chron. 32.9 and Isa. 36.2; 37.8).[35] The lament of
Mic. 1.8-16 probably also originates from the time of the Assyrian
conquest of 701, since here Lachish is mentioned among the places to
be mourned for.[36] The great significance of this military victory for
Sennacherib is demonstrated by the fact that the capture of Lachish was
depicted in reliefs in his palace at Nineveh. Lachish was certainly
the most important city in Judah after Jerusalem: after its fall Hiskia
(725–697) bought his freedom by paying a ransom, in order to spare
the capital city the fate of a siege and storming by the Assyrians (cf.
2 Kgs 18.14-18).

Lachish is the only city in Judah and Israel that is depicted in Assyrian
reliefs (fig. 37).[37] In a sequence of scenes, the attack by infantry, the
storming and the defence of the city walls, the leading away of prisoners
and booty, Sennacherib on his throne, the king's tent and war chariot as
well as the Assyrian camp are shown. The representation of the city with

34. The listing of Lachish amongst the forts of Rehoboam in 2 Chron. 11.5-10
can be ignored in this context, since this list probably only dates from a later time.
Cf. V. Fritz, 'The "List of Rehoboam's Fortresses" in 2 Chronicles 11.5-12. A
Document from the Time of Josiah', *Eretz Israel* 15 (1981), pp. 46*-53*; N. Na'aman,
'Hezekiah's Fortified Cities and the *LMLK* Stamp', *BASOR* 261 (1986), pp. 5-21.

35. On the historical events that took place beforehand cf. N. Na'aman,
'Sennacherib's "Letter to God" on his Campaign to Judah', *BASOR* 214 (1974),
pp. 25-39; also 'Sennacherib's Campaign to Judah and the Date of the *lmlk* Stamps',
VT 29 (1979), pp. 61-86; D. Ussishkin, 'The Destruction of Lachish by Sennacherib
and the Dating of the Royal Judean Storage Jars', *Tel Aviv* 4 (1977), pp. 28-60;
A.F. Rainey, 'The Fate of Lachish during the Campaigns of Sennacherib and
Nebuchadnezzar', in Y. Aharoni, *Investigations at Lachish* (1975), pp. 47-60.

36. Cf. here K. Elliger, 'Die Heimat des Propheten Micha', *ZDPV* 57 (1934),
pp. 81-152 = *Kleine Schriften zum Alten Testament* (1966), pp. 9-71.

37. Published by D. Ussishkin, *The Conquest of Lachish by Sennacherib* (1982).

its walls and the towers jutting out above them was executed according to the Assyrian pictorial ideal, as was the attack by the infantry, assisted by siege machines,[38] but in spite of that the reliefs give a good impression of what an Israelite city looked like. Together with the results of the excavations they permit a reconstruction of the character of the city (fig. 38). The ramp thrown up by the Assyrians for the storming of the city can still be seen in the south-western corner, in the form of a huge pile of stones. There is a corresponding ramp inside the city to meet the threat thus posed. Little is known about the city of the seventh century (Stratum II). It is probable that after the eclipse of the Assyrian domination the city was resettled and surrounded once more by a wall; in addition a new gate complex was built. The palace area was also probably reused, but the city did not attain its former strength and importance again. The final destruction of Lachish took place at the hands of

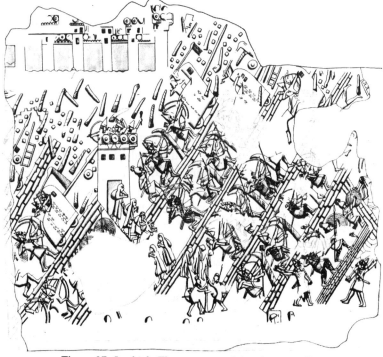

Figure 37. *Lachish. The conquest of the city according
to the relief of Sanherib in Ninive.*

38. Cf. R.D. Barnett, 'The Siege of Lachish', *IEJ* 8 (1958), pp. 161-64; D. Ussishkin, 'The "Lachish Reliefs" and the City of Lachish', *IEJ* 30 (1980), pp. 174-95.

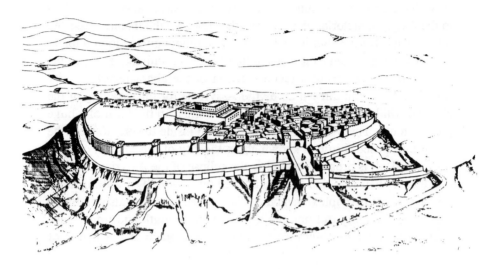

Figure 38. *Lachish. Reconstruction of the city in Stratum III.*

Nebuchadnezzar in 587 along with numerous other places in Judah, including the capital city, Jerusalem.

Tell Beit Mirsim

The name of the city on *Tell Beit Mirsim* is unknown, but can be looked for among those of the third district in the Shefela in Josh. 15.37-41; this district was probably administered from Lachish. The site was settled for the first time towards the end of the third millennium. There was a city there from Middle Bronze Age II B onwards, and its tradition continued on into Iron Age I.[39] The city of Iron Age II was probably first founded after 926 (Stratum A) but it did not survive the Assyrian conquests at the end of the eighth century and was abandoned before 700.

The Iron Age city (fig. 39) was relatively large, with an area of almost 5 hectares.[40] The city gate was in the south-east, but cannot be reconstructed with any certainty. Of the double ring of walls, the external wall measures 1.8 m in width, and is wider than the inner wall.

39. Now cf. R. Greenberg, 'New Light on the Early Iron Age at Tell Beit Mirsim', *BASOR* 265 (1987), pp. 55-80.

40. W.F. Albright, *Excavation of Tell Beit Mirsim III. The Iron Age* (AASOR 21/22; 1943).

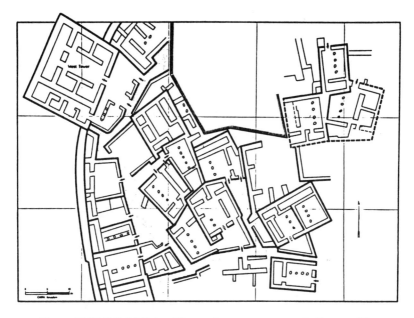

Figure 39. Tell Beit Misim. *The north-western quarter in Stratum III.*

The spaces created between them were widely integrated into the houses which abutted onto the walls. The so-called three-room house predominates, but there are also houses which are divided up by one or two rows of pillars, and four-room houses in several variations. A conspicuous attempt had been made to extend the house through the addition of a forecourt. An especially large four-room house projected out in tower-like fashion from the city wall. The street plan is extremely irregular. A street ran alongside the houses which were situated along the wall, but it is not possible to speak of a 'ring road' following a completely parallel course. Thus a picture is presented of a residential city with a pattern of streets placed at all angles to one another, and behind which no orderly principle of planning of any kind can be recognized.

Tell es-Seba'

The city on *Tell es-Seba'* is a direct successor of the Early Iron Age settlement on the hill (Strata IX–VI). Its identification with the biblical Beersheba is by no means attested and thus will not be considered here. There are basically two settlements to be differentiated, each of which

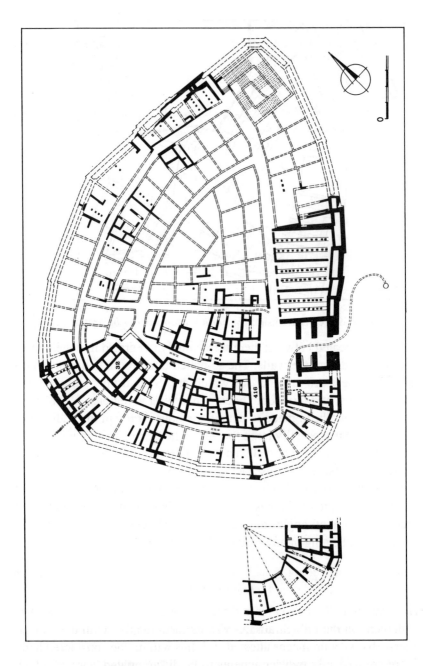

Figure 40. Tell es-Seba'. *The city in Stratum II.*

exhibits signs of two phases of building activity.[41] Until now, only sparse remains of the older city of Strata V and IV, dating to the second half of the tenth century and the ninth century, have been uncovered. By contrast, the later city of Strata III and II, dating from the eighth century, has been excavated to such an extent that the layout of the whole city is clear (figs. 40 and 41).

With its projecting and recessed sections the casemate wall encloses an area of around 1 hectare; the mud-brick wall was constructed on a stone foundation. Entrance to the city was through a four-chamber gate on the southern side and led to an open square in the centre of the city. This square is the starting point for a clearly discernible system of streets. Although the 'ring road' has not been completely uncovered, its planned course parallel to the city wall can be clearly recognized. Two additional service roads divide the buildings into individual blocks or segments, of which two in the western sector have been almost completely excavated. Even when the directions in which the streets ran in the north-eastern half of the city remain hypothetical, the courses of the streets that have been discerned to date indicate an underlying plan which ensured the best possible accessibility of every point within the city from the city gate. There is a complete absence of the cul-de-sac, since access roads secured the entryway into each house through good layout.

This effective planning ensured the drainage of the city. There were long channels beneath the streets, which were paved with flat stones; these channels came together at the city gate and led to the outside beneath the passage through it. Surface water could also run away via the roads through the gate.

The buildings were mostly private houses, whose ground-plans exhibited the numerous variations in Israelite building form. There were only minimal differences in size between the houses. The houses situated on the ring road incorporated the spaces within the casemate wall so that there are occasionally irregular ground plans, without the principles of orderly planning being breached (fig. 42). Because of the strict pattern of streets only few houses gained additional courtyard space. Over the

41. The following reports exist for the excavations carried out between 1969 and 1976: *Beer-Sheba I. Excavations at Tel Beer-sheba, 1969–71 Seasons* (ed. Y. Aharoni; 1973); Y. Aharoni, 'Excavations at Tel Beer-sheba, Preliminary Report of the Fourth Season, 1972', *Tel Aviv* 1 (1974), pp. 34-42 and 'Preliminary Report of the Fifth and Sixth Seasons 1973-4', *Tel Aviv* 2 (1975), pp. 146-68.

Figure 41. Tell es-Seba'. *The excavated parts of the city of the Iron Age II.*

area as a whole only few houses stand out, as for example the house
next to the gate and house 32 in the west. Both were probably inhabited
by officials, whose elevated social status manifested itself in the way in
which the houses were constructed, without the usual building form
being abandoned. Two buildings with an official function were situated
in the immediate vicinity of the gate. There is an adjacent complex with
three pillar-houses in the north east; these houses were positioned at a
right angle to the wall (fig. 43). These were quarters for the troops, who
were connected with the military security of the kingdom. The building
with three parallel long rooms to the west of the gate (41b) was most
likely used for the storage and administration of taxes paid in kind. No
palace-type complex has been found to date; the officials empowered to
issue orders or act as supervisors most likely lived in the two private
houses which were given special mention above because of their size. A
shaft for the purpose of supplying water was detected in the the eastern
corner, but only recently completely excavated.

Figure 42. Tell es-Seba'. *The living quarters at the western edge of the city.*

Figure 43. Tell es-Seba'. *The pillar-houses beside the gate.*

Due to the find of several stones from a horned altar, which were secondarily reused in the walls of Stratum II, the question arises as to whether there was a temple inside the city. The location of the altar in the house to the south-west of the gate, as suggested by Y. Yadin, is thus totally out of the question, since this house is clearly a private residence.[42] The assumption of Y. Aharoni that the temple stood on the site of house 32[43] cannot be proved, since this house was built on and thus all earlier occupation layers were destroyed. However, this theory is supported by both the east-west axis of the site and the later situation of a Hellenistic temple there.

The city on *Tell es-Seba'* had a well-conceived, structured layout which developed out of the oval shape of the city. Important elements are the positioning of houses in rows along the city wall, the bringing together of houses to form blocks, and the strict orientation of the walls of the houses on the sides of streets. Both the first two elements are also occasionally found in other Israelite cities, but could not prevent the usual formation of building agglomerations. It was only adherence to a preplanned network of streets that produced the well-ordered whole, whose outward appearance is that of a city with planning behind it.

Tell es-Sa'idīyeh

Tell es-Sa'idīyeh lies in the middle of the Jordan valley, on the east bank; its ancient name is unknown. The place was already inhabited in the Early Bronze Age, but at present just as little is known about the site as about the whole history of settlement there.[44] A cemetery dating to the end of the Late Bronze Age has been partly excavated but no settlement belonging to it has been discovered so far. Three settlement levels of Iron Age II can be distinguished (Strata VII–V).[45]

The city of Stratum VII was surrounded by a wall 3.5 m wide. The houses which directly abutted onto it in general consisted of only two rooms and were relatively small. The impoverished aspect of the buildings indicates that this was a residential quarter for the lower

42. As opposed to Y. Yadin, 'Beer-sheba: The High Place Destroyed by King Josiah', *BASOR* 222 (1976), pp. 5-17 cf. the correction by Z. Herzog, A.F. Rainey and Sh. Moshkovitz, 'The Stratigraphy at Beer-sheba and the Location of the Sanctuary', *BASOR* 225 (1977), pp. 49-58.

43. Y. Aharoni, *Tel Aviv* 2 (1975), pp. 158-65.

44. J.B. Pritchard, *Tell es-Sa'idiyeh. Excavations on the Tell, 1964–66* (Philadelphia, 1985).

45. The latest excavations were able to trace the history of the settlement back into the eleventh century (Strata VIII–XII), cf. J.N. Tubb, 'Tell es-Sa'idiyeh: Preliminary Report on the First Three Seasons of Renewed Excavations', *Levant* 20 (1988), pp. 23-73.

classes. Stratum VII is to be assigned to the end of the ninth century, without a more exact dating being possible. In the following occupation level residential buildings were constructed over the city wall; thus Stratum VI must be considered an unfortified settlement. The houses consisted of a square room whose sides measured 4.5 m in length, but as the latter was too wide to be completely roofed over, there is a possibility that it was subdivided by a row of pillars; this may also be indicated by the fact that paving was found only on one half of the floor.

The city was refortified at the time of the new construction in Stratum V. However, the city wall was only 1.5 m wide, but was reinforced with towers projecting 1 m out from the wall at regular distances, for the purpose of better defensibility. The building that was carried on within the walls is extremely regular in nature. Not only are the three-room houses of almost the same size and exhibit the same subdivision into rooms, but they were also set next to each other in rows so that two rows of five houses each, with their back rooms touching each other, constitute a block (fig. 44). The creation of this *insula* measuring about 38 x 18 m is clearly the result of prior planning. The building units are partly destroyed at the northern and southern ends, but the reconstruction is corroborated by the remains that are left. The streets running alongside the block in the east and west were between 1 and 1.8 m wide and paved with small stones, and were crossed at right angles by streets running parallel to the city wall. The continuation of the buildings in a southern direction indicates that the *insulae* could vary in size, so that the roads do not constitute, as it were, the strings in a network of regular appearance, but one in which they meet each other in an irregular pattern.

The city was built during the course of the eighth century and destroyed during the Assyrian conquest of 734/3. After that, it was not rebuilt. The numerous pits hollowed into the debris for storage purposes can be dated on the grounds of pottery to the end of the eighth century, and indicate sporadic habitation of the tell, without new building activities having taken place.

Summary

Apart from the capital cities, which occupy a special position and will be dealt with separately in Chapter 6, the various cities definitely exhibit

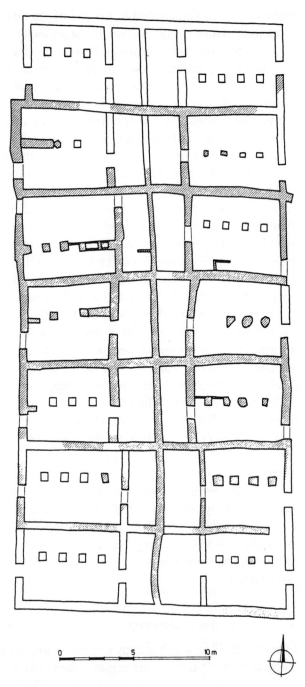

Figure 44. Tell es-Seba'. *Living quarter of Stratum V.*

certain differences in their external appearance. Using the degree to which controlled planning has replaced uncontrolled growth as a scale, the cities of Israel that have been excavated to date can be divided into three groups, on the basis of the characteristic differences they exhibit:

1. *The Residential City*

The residential city is devoid of any planning, and the houses stood close together in the form of an agglomeration. Public buildings were completely absent. The streets followed an irregular course without orientation towards the gate. Examples of this type of city are Mizpa and the city on *Tell Beit Mirsim*.

2. *The City with a Limited Administrative or Military Function*

This type differs from the residential city in its careful planning, as can be seen in Stratum II at Kinneret or on *Tell es-Seba'* Stratum II. A limited number of public buildings are situated near the city gate. The houses are carefully arranged in rows or in blocks so that, apart from the ring road which follows the course of the city wall, the streets are broadly orientated in a straight line. Most of the streets open into a square in front of the city gate. Although the larger part of the area is covered by private houses, the city clearly had a further function in that, at the same time, it played a certain role in the administration or defence of the country. Its layout was derived from a schematic plan which was hardly a local development, but rather laid down by a central authority. The plans were probably drawn up by an office attached to the royal palace and their execution watched over on the site, with individual elements originating from ancient Israelite building tradition. Only the position of the public buildings and the alignment of the streets were stipulated. By contrast there was no standardization of the limits of building where individual houses were concerned, so that in individual blocks of streets a certain variety is visible in the house types. A prototype for this type of city has not been discerned up to the present.

3. *The City as an Administrative or Military Centre*

These cities were built for the purpose of administration and defence of the kingdom. Although there were a certain number of private houses in them, the large official buildings were clearly of most importance. This is shown in different ways by the two single examples of Megiddo and Lachish. In Megiddo Stratum IV B, the pillar-house complexes take up most of the available space, a fact which most likely points to the stationing of troops. A large palace with outbuildings is at the centre of Lachish Stratum IV, and this can most likely be considered as the seat of the city governor. In both cases a close connection with the palace administration can be presupposed. Apart from the fact that the positioning of the large official buildings was the result of planning, there are no further signs of structured layout in the rest of the city; however, the excavated areas are all extremely small. Through the supremacy of their position, the public buildings dominate the city to such an extent that every further building erected occupied a subordinate position.

The ancient Israelite city is thus by no means of a consistent size, and each of the various layouts reflects a different function. The various forms represent different concepts: the residential city has its roots back in the settlement form of the village, which developed as a simple agglomeration of residential houses. The limitation of the area which could be built upon necessitated a greater closeness of buildings and a correspondingly convoluted network of streets. In the city which fulfilled an administrative or military role a network of streets was established which gave, to a certain degree, a clear planned aspect to the city; this was in addition to the construction of buildings necessary for the tasks which had been set down and assumed by the monarchy. By contrast the division into units according to a rectangular street pattern which was carried out in Megiddo Stratum III is not Israelite, but must be assigned to Assyrian influences. A third type was represented by such cities which were totally in the service of the monarchy, whether on military or economic grounds. This city is characterized by its public buildings, accordingly located at its centre, while a lesser degree of planning was afforded to the rest of the site.

The various types are represented in the cities of the ninth and eighth centuries and develop fully in this period. Whether they already existed in this form during the united kingdom of the tenth century is at present beyond our knowledge. A city with a limited administrative or military function is already attested in Megiddo Stratum V A, even if an orderly network of streets is lacking. The enlargement of the city into an administrative or military centre seems first to have taken place in the period after the division of the kingdom, as both the demands of kingship and the possibilities offered by it had increased.

In spite of all the differences there are also a number of common features. The cities are to a greater or lesser degree oval in form, a fact which is to be put down to the outline of the sites. They are situated on a tell or on a hilltop; positions on a slope as in the case of Kinneret Stratum V are the exception. The city is surrounded by a strong ring of walls, whereby various types of fortification could be used. There was generally only one gate which due to the lack of other buildings also had a simultaneous civil function. In domestic building the typical Israelite constructional forms of the pillar-, three- and four-room houses are predominant. Numerous cities were provided with their own systems of water supply, which represented significant technical achievements (cf. below, Chapter 8).

At the same time the cities differed radically from the Early Iron Age settlements, even if these employed the same house forms in domestic building. The difference not only lies in the fact that the cities were protected by a wall, but the construction of the fortifications also had consequences where the arrangement of other buildings was concerned. While the villages could spread at will, the city was limited to the area enclosed by the wall. However, the villages of the eleventh century, such as Ai, *Tell es-Seba'* Stratum VII or *Khirbet el-Meshâsh* Stratum II already exhibit a certain closed appearance in their layout (cf. figs. 15, 21, 24), so that a closed facade of houses is formed on the edge of the village, even with all the irregularity in building that is apparent. It cannot however be assumed that the Israelite city developed as it were from the Early Iron Age village.[46] The construction of a fortification is a completely new element, which does not change the method of building the houses or their arrangement, but does necessitate a new form of layout and settlement.

On the one hand, the closed ring of a wall enforces the necessity of an effective usage of the fortified area, while on the other the buildings must be aligned and positioned in such a way that all houses can be reached from the city gate, which functions as the only access. This necessity obliges the streets to follow a course either along or parallel to the city wall; this so-called 'ring road' is the most conspicuous element of planning in the Israelite residential city. The houses in the centre of the city area could be reached by means of access roads, of which most were culs-de-sac. This principle could not be adhered to in administrative

46. Such a connection is implied by Y. Shiloh, 'Elements in the Development of Town Planning in the Israelite City', *IEJ* 28 (1978), pp. 36-51, when he postulates a connection between the arrangement in rows of three- and four-room houses on the edge of the town and the casemate wall. Against this is the fact that the casemate wall is already met as an independent structure in Hazor as early as the tenth century.

or military centres, since large areas were taken up for public buildings with streets leading down to them from the city gate; here the various buildings could either be in the centre, as at Lachish, or along the city wall as in Megiddo Stratum IV B.

Since the beginning of urbanization the city wall has been a necessary element of the city defences. In the period of Early Bronze Age II and III, just as during the Middle and Late Bronze Ages, the newly-founded cities were protected by a system of walls, which often reached gigantic dimensions. But during the Late Bronze Age, however, a few of the cities, such as Megiddo or Gezer, were left without a protective ring of walls. The reasons for this are unknown but this lack can in no way be put down to the political conditions of the time, since this period was not exactly a very peaceful one. The fortification of a settlement during the Early Iron Age was rather the exception, but it became the rule at the beginning of the Iron Age II in the tenth century. Here, from the beginning, both systems of massive walls and casemate walls existed side by side.

The cities founded from the beginning of the period of the monarchy onwards are thus not the result of a continuous development, but exhibit an underlying planned concept. Only a state desirous of expansion has to take into account the need to defend itself and carry out the appropriate protective measures. The new phase of urbanization which occurred together with the building of the state in Israel bears clear signs of a political desire for planning. The settlement is fitted into a ring of walls, in order to ensure the inhabitants of the safety which would be necessary in time of war. The technical details of construction are drawn from the building tradition of the country and the environment (cf. below, Chapter 7). Because the house types were retained, the city only differed from the village—apart from the fact that it was fortified— through the greater density of building that took place there. Due to this fact, during the course of history, the layout of the city was determined according to basic principles. An altered planning concept is only visible in the cities which served an administrative or military function and in the capital cities, since their greater role, as reflected in the buildings in them, necessitated new planning.

Chapter 6

CAPITAL CITIES AND RESIDENCES

The establishment of the monarchy in Israel poses the question of a royal residence, that is to say, not only a private residence fit for the king and his court, but an establishment large enough to house the administration. Although documents relating to this have not survived, the small number of letters from the fortress of Arad show that the king and his representatives ruled in every place in the kingdom and made the necessary decisions in all matters.[1] In addition, the ostraka from Samaria indicate an extremely pernickety bookkeeping where the receipt of deliveries of oil and wine to the royal court were concerned.[2] This glimpse of practice permits recognition of an effective system for the transmission of orders and the carrying out of the administration during the period of the monarchy.

Saul, who reigned until 1004, remained in Gibea, the place of his birth, after his elevation to the kingship (1 Sam. 10.26; 11.4; 15.34; 22.6). Gibea can be identified with *Tell el-Fūl*.[3] David reigned as king of Judah in Hebron for seven years (2 Sam. 5.5). Only after the extension of his rule over all the northern tribes and the capture of Jerusalem did he first begin to build up the city and made it the new capital of the kingdom (2 Sam. 5.6-9). Solomon then made a firm contribution to this development by building a new palace and temple (1 Kgs 6 and 7).

After the division of the kingdom Jerusalem remained the capital city of Judah until it was conquered by the Babylonians in 587. During the reigns of the later kings of the dynasty of David only sporadic building

---

1. Cf. Y. Aharoni, *Arad Inscriptions* (1981).
2. Cf. Aharoni, *The Land of the Bible*, pp. 356-68.
3. The excavations on *Tell el-Fūl* revealed nothing about the prestate settlement. The dating of a fort to the time of Saul seems to be out of the question in view of the type of construction, contra L.A. Sinclair, 'An Archaeological Study of Gibeah (Tell el-Fûl)', *AASOR* 34/35 (1960), pp. 1-52.

activities were mentioned; these were limited to the measures necessary for the maintenance of the temple. The kings of the northern kingdom of Israel changed the location of their residence several times. At first, Jeroboam (926–907) reigned in Shechem (1 Kgs 12.25), but then transferred his residence to Tirza (cf. 1 Kgs 14.17). Omri (878–871) built a new capital city, Samaria, which remained the focal point of the kingdom until the conquest in 722.

Not only do the biblical sources provide numerous references to the two capitals Jerusalem and Samaria but they have also been examined by excavation. Even if the written and archaeological sources for the history and layout of these two cities with royal residences do not give a complete picture, their particular role is made adequately clear.

Jerusalem

Jerusalem was founded during Middle Bronze Age II A and is already mentioned in the later group of Execration Texts.[4] The Canaanite city also held sway over the villages in the vicinity, but the actual area of influence cannot be defined more clearly. Letters from its king Abdi-Hepa to the Pharaoh from the archive in Amarna (EA 285-290) indicate that the the neighbouring city states of Shechem, Gezer and Hebron carried on a policy of encirclement, in order to weaken the influence of Jerusalem. Whether this critical situation in the middle of the fourteenth century was brought to an end by Egyptian intervention lies outside our knowledge. Jerusalem apparently survived the downfall of the Canaanite cities unscathed, since it was still intact at the time of its conquest by David.[5] It is possible that other names of the city's kings were preserved in the names Melchizedek (Gen. 14.18) and Adonizedek (Josh. 10.3; Judg. 1.5ff.), but no definite proof can be offered.

The report of the taking of Jerusalem by David in 2 Sam. 5.6-9 is obscure; the capture may have been brought about by a strategem. The building up of the city by David is only given brief mention in 2 Sam. 5.9, without any details. The Millo mentioned in this connection, just as the palace in 2 Sam. 5.11, probably refers to building measures undertaken by Solomon but attributed to his predecessor, David. The new capital enjoyed a favourable geographical position on the border

---

4.   G. Posener, *Princes et pays d'Asie et de Nubie* (1940), Nr. 45.

5.   For the history of Jerusalem cf. E. Otto, *Jerusalem—die Geschichte der Heiligen Stadt* (1980).

between Judah and the northern tribes. As a result of the conquest, David joined the line of succession of the subsequent kings of the city and thus acquired, along with the supremacy over the tribes, the rights as ruler of the city-state.[6] This position was an important prerequisite for the building measures carried out by Solomon.

The building of the temple and palace in Jerusalem by Solomon is described in detail in 1 Kings 6 and 7. The great construction programme in the capital could only be carried out with the employment of Phoenician craftsmen and the use of enforced labour (cf. 1 Kgs 7.52 and 5.27). In addition there was the delivery of wood for building from the Lebanon (1 Kgs 5.15-26) and the use of bronze for the decoration and embellishments of the temple (1 Kgs 7.13-47). The debts incurred thereby were settled by the cession of the land of Kabul—probably a name for the Plain of Akko (Acre)—to Hyram of Tyre (1 Kgs 9.10-14).

The royal palace was probably situated north of the Davidic city, since the city precinct could only have extended in this direction. The discovery of remains of this site can never be expected, because they were destroyed during the extension of the temple square at the time of Herod. According to the description in 1 Kgs 7.1-12, the royal palace comprised the following parts: a house of the forest of Lebanon, a hall of columns with a vestibule hall, a throne room, residential quarters and a palace for the women. The brevity of the description does not permit a reconstruction of the parts named, but the great extent, the high quality of construction and the separation of official and residential parts are all clear.[7] In addition, extensive courts are also to be presupposed, even though they are not mentioned by name. In contrast to the city, the palace formed a completely independent unit, which was surrounded by its own wall and thus separated from the city. Nothing is mentioned of the previous palace or its continued use. The Millo created by Solomon (1 Kgs 9.15, 24; 11.27) presumably refers to a further acquisition of land through terracing or to an extension of the city northwards.[8]

6.   On the legal position of the king cf. A. Alt, *Das Königtum in den Reichen Israel und Juda, Kleine Schriften zur Geschichte des Volkes Israel*, II (2nd edn, 1959), pp. 116-34.

7.   Cf. D. Ussishkin, 'King Solomon's Palaces', *BA* 36 (1973), pp. 78-105.

8.   The puzzling expression *millo'* is still unexplained, in spite of all attempts made. The most likely explanation has to do with the filling-in of the hollow between the former Canaanite city and the palace complex in the area of the modern Temple Square, cf. L.E. Stager 'The Archaeology of the East Slope of Jerusalem and the Terraces of Kidron', *JNES* 41 (1982), pp. 111-24.

The temple was situated within the area of palace, and was thus a royal sanctuary.[9] According to 1 Kgs 6.2, 3 this was a long-room temple with a vestibule hall and a separate compartment for the Holy of Holies, which most probably was a wooden construction.[10] Two columns stood in the vestibule hall between extended longitudinal walls, so that the form of a temple *in antes* was created (cf. Fig. 50).[11] Thus the plan follows the form of the so-called north Syrian type of temple, which has been identified in the second millennium in several locations in northern Syria, and was still used in the eighth century on *Tell Ta'yīnāt*.[12] Even if the long-room temple was common in Canaan in the second millennium (cf. fig. 5–7), a direct derivation from Canaanite building tradition is questionable, since this form of building could also have been brought in by the Phoenicians. At any rate, this is a non-Israelite type of temple whose form was taken over by Solomon.

The description of the fittings and furnishings given in 1 Kgs 7.13-50 indicates that this was a splendid edifice, decorated with ancient eastern pictorial motifs. The walls were panelled with wood and covered in gold foil. The carved cherubims, palms and entwined floral motifs were probably pictorial embellishments executed in semi-relief. It was also furnished with cultic equipment of extreme splendour. Most of the objects, such as the molten sea, the cauldrons with their stands, vessels, spades and sprinkler vessels were cast in bronze. The two columns in the vestibule hall, which were probably made of wood, were given a covering of sheet bronze. As in the case of the ground plan, the furnishings and fittings of the temple also exhibit an extra-Israelite influence, which

9.   On the temple cf. T.A. Busink, *Der Tempel von Jerusalem von Salomo bis Herodes*, I (1970), und II (1980); V. Fritz, 'Der Tempel Salomos im Licht der neueren Forschung', *MDOG* 112 (1980), pp. 53-68; H. Schmid, 'Der Tempelbau Salomos in religionsgeschichtlicher Sicht', in *Archäologie und Altes Testament, Festschrift K. Galling* (1970), pp. 241-50.

10.   Cf. H. Schult, 'Der Debir im Salomonischen Tempel', *ZDPV* 80 (1964), pp. 46-54.

11.   The position of the columns is disputed, but their location *in antes* is the only reasonable interpretation of the statement in 1 Kgs 7.21, cf. V. Fritz, *Tempel und Zelt* (1977), pp. 14-15. The annexed building described in 1 Kgs 6.6-8 is of secondary literary and constructional importance, cf. K. Rupprecht, 'Nachrichten von Erweiterung und Renovierung des Tempels in 1 Kings 6', *ZDPV* 88 (1972), pp. 38-52.

12.   R.C. Haines, *Excavations in the Plain of Antioch, II. The Structural Remains of the Later Phases* (1971), pp. 53-55, Pl. 103.

far surpasses local craftsmanship and places it on a par with other ancient temple complexes in the Levant.

No further building activities are reported where the later kings of the dynasty of David are concerned; they only carried out the works necessary for the maintenance or restoration of the temple. The only larger building measures were undertaken at the time of Hiskia when a tunnel was hewn through the rock, by means of which the water from the spring of Gihon was brought into the city (2 Kgs 20.20). The sources are otherwise silent, and in particular provide no information about the construction of a new quarter of the city called *mišnaeh*—'Second' (cf. 2 Kgs 22.14; Zeph. 1.10; 2 Chron. 34.22). However, on the grounds of topographical evidence, this could only have been situated on the southwestern hill. Thus the later constructional development of the city can only be determined by archaeological excavation.

The Canaanite city occupied a spur position on the south-eastern hill, which is outside the city wall that encloses the Old City today.[13] The spur is situated between two deep valleys, which meet at its southern end; these are the Kidron Valley in the east and the Tyropoeon Valley on the western side. This valley in the west could have been that alluded to by the name *maktes*, 'the mortar', in Zeph. 1.11. The terrain continued to rise up towards the north until it reached the rock on which the Dome of the Rock is situated today as its highest point. This location was determined by the presence of the spring situated at the foot of the eastern slope; this spring produces an extraordinary amount of water the whole year round and bears the name Gihon in 1 Kgs 1.33, 38, 45 and 2 Chron. 32.30; 33.14.

Although pre-Hellenistic Jerusalem could only be examined in places up till now, the limits of the city have been broadly established (fig. 45). The predecessor of the city founded in Middle Bronze Age II A was an Early Bronze Age settlement, the existence of which is only indicated by pottery finds.[14] The Middle Bronze Age city wall was built on the eastern side, on the lower part of the slope, and enclosed an area of about

13. On the topography cf. G. Dalman, *Jerusalem und sein Gelände* (1930); J. Simons, *Jerusalem in the Old Testament* (1952).

14. Cf. R. Amiran, *Ancient Pottery of the Holy Land* (1969), Pl. 11: 8.9.12; R.S. Macalister and J.G. Duncan, *Excavations on the Hill of Ophel, Jerusalem 1923-25* (PEFA IV; 1926), pp. 174ff.

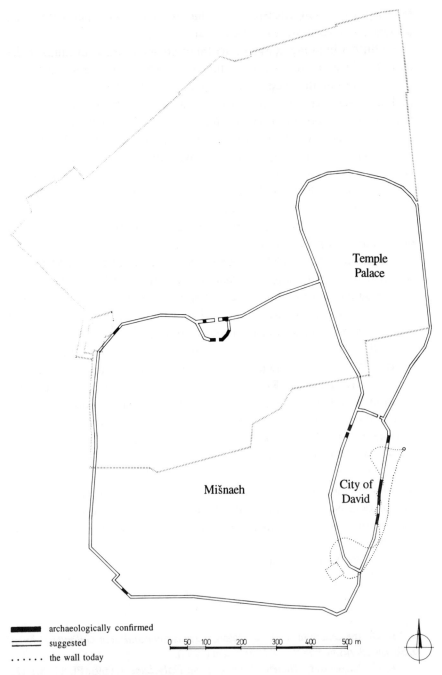

Figure 45. *Jerusalem. The city at the end of the monarchy.*

4 hectares; however, its course on the northern side is unknown.[15] Its width fluctuates strongly because of its projecting and recessed sections. It was impossible to establish how long this wall was in use during the Late Bronze Age. The city wall of the early Period of the Monarchy sits directly on top of this wall; thus the Israelite city corresponded in extent to that of the Canaanite city. The course followed by the fortifications led to the enforced location of buildings on the steep slope, but these were given special security by a form of *glacis* or ramp. The private houses were thus situated on terraces, with the ancient Israelite type of building being retained as far as possible.[16] In view of the pressing restriction of space in the city, it must be assumed that the palace of Solomon, together with the temple, was situated in the north of the city, in the area of the second temple whose limits are still defined today by the enclosing wall of Herod.

It was only around 700 that the construction of a new city wall took place on the eastern slope, a little above the course followed by the previous wall. As this building activity is not mentioned in the Books of the Kings, it is impossible to date it more closely, but it may be connected with the building operations carried out to improve the water supply at the time of Hiskia (725–697). The incorporation of the south-west hill into the city precinct also took place in the same period; the area of the latter was thus increased to about 60 hectares (fig. 45). This area of the south-eastern hill was already sporadically inhabited during the eighth century, since the space inside the walls had apparently become too crowded. Only the discovery of two sections of wall on the northern edge and in the north-west corner of the settlement area provided proof that this new city called called Mišnaeh was fortified during the seventh century. The further course of this wall in the west and the south is not demonstrated with certainty by any other remnants of wall, but can be ascertained on topographical grounds.[17] Thus, Jerusalem achieved its

15. On the archaeological examination cf. K. Kenyon, *Jerusalem: Die heilige Stadt von David bis zu den Kreuzzügen. Ausgrabungen 1961–7* (1968); Y. Yadin (ed.), *Jerusalem Revealed. Archaeology Discovering Jerusalem* (1983); N. Avigad, *Discovering Jerusalem* (1983); Y. Shiloh, *Excavations at the City of David I, 1978–82* (Qedem 19; 1984).

16. Cf. the so-called 'Haus des Ahiel', in Y. Shiloh, *Excavations at the City of David I*, fig. 25.

17. Cf. M. Broshi, 'The Expansion of Jerusalem in the Reigns of Hezekiah and Manasseh', *IEJ* 24 (1974), pp. 21-26; H. Geva, 'The Western Boundary of Jerusalem at the End of the Monarchy', *IEJ* 29 (1979), pp. 84-91.

greatest extent and highest density of population in the period of the monarchy. The importance of Jerusalem as the capital city of Judah was now also reflected in the size of the area occupied.

Samaria

A certain number of building measures were connected with the choice of Shechem as the new capital city of the northern kingdom of Israel by Jeroboam (1 Kgs 12.25). Whether these included a palace as well as the fortifications lies beyond our knowledge. The further relocation of the royal residence to Tirza is passed over in silence in the biblical sources. Of the successors of Jeroboam only Baesa (906–883) ruled long enough to undertake the necessary further building. The royal palace at Tirza is only mentioned in 1 Kgs 16.18. The reason why Omri (878–871) refounded the capital city once again can only be guessed at from the short note in 1 Kgs 16.23f., which states that:

> It was in the thirty-first year of Asa king of Judah that Omri became king of Israel and he reigned twelve years, six of them in Tirzah. He bought the hill of Samaria from Shemer for two talents of silver and built a city on it which he named Samaria after Shemer the owner of the hill.

With the purchase the site passed into royal ownership and was thus subject to royal power and jurisdiction. As in the case of Davidic Jerusalem, Samaria belonged to the Omrids and their successors.

From the very beginning, a comprehensive building programme was connected with the choice of the new residence. The hill chosen by the king was completely devoid of buildings, with the exception of a few farmsteads. The isolated hill of Samaria controlled the access to the Mountains of Ephraim from the coastal plain and included a plateau of about 8 hectares in area. The view from the western tip extended as far as the Mediterranean. The total area of the city has not yet been determined, but a part of the acropolis has been excavated (fig. 46). In accordance with the topography of the site this forms a lengthwise extended rectangle, which has an almost west-east orientation. On the evidence of the finds from excavation, two building phases are to be differentiated, of which the older belongs to the reign of Omri, while the extension can be assigned to his successor Ahab.[18]

18. There is a summary with bibliography in H. Weippert, *Palästina in vor-hellenistischer Zeit* (1988), pp. 535-40.

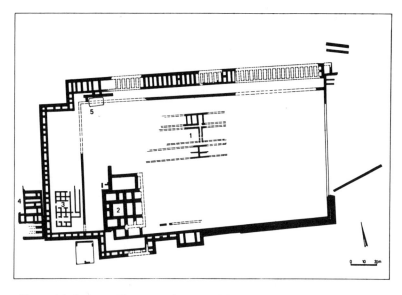

Figure 46. *Samaria. The acropolis: 1. Building with finds of ivory. 2. Palace. 3. House of the ostraca. 4. Additional structure. 5. Basin.*

In the first phase the precinct of 178 × 89 m was surrounded by a wall 1.5–1.6 m wide, which simultaneously served as a retaining wall for the material that was of necessity deposited there. The retaining wall, just like all of the buildings inside it, was constructed of carefully prepared ashlar blocks. The palace (fig. 46.2) was situated on the west side, but the ground plan could only be partly established. In the area which has been preserved the rooms are arranged around a court measuring 8.4 × 9.5 m, and there was an adjoining court in the north. The continuation in northern and eastern directions has not been preserved. In its layout, this palace with its subdivision through central courts follows Canaanite building tradition. The remains further to the north-east must be seen as those of an independent building complex because of the different thickness of the walls. In spite of the ivory objects found here, a purpose cannot be assigned to the complex, as the remains are too sparse.[19] Other buildings have not been preserved; access was from the east, where the location of a gate inside the encircling wall can be assumed.

19. Since the ivory sculptures do not constitute building decorations, they will not be mentioned in more detail in this connection; cf. J.W. Crowfoot and G.M. Crowfoot, *Early Ivories from Samaria* (1938).

The existence of several courts situated between the individual buildings is also likely.

During a second phase, the acropolis was enlarged to dimensions of almost 200 × 100 m and enclosed by a casemate wall, the thickness of which fluctuates considerably. This enlargement necessitated further deposition of fill and was also apparently carried out with defensive measures in view. Further protection was afforded by a tower on the south side, which was probably accessible from the acropolis wall. The palace and the building in the northern half continued in use. An administrative building was constructed in the segment gained by this expansion on the west side; this building broadly resembles building 1482 in Megiddo Stratum V A (fig. 46.3). It consists of a total of three units, in which the rooms are located along the long side of a court, as in the pillar-house, with halls situated at an oblique angle to them.[20] The pottery found here indicates that the building had an official function, although it remains an open question whether deliveries of crown property or goods paid as taxes were stored there. Another building outside the western boundary wall (fig. 46.4) probably marks a further, third phase of building; this building seems to have been surrounded by a type of casemate wall, and it most likely served as a private house.

The acropolis of Samaria thus had a double function. As an independent and fortified area it attested to the particular position held by the king and provided a location for the palace. In addition there were also buildings connected with the royal administration within its precincts, from which both the provisioning of the royal house and the government of the kingdom could be supervised. The acropolis constituted the centre of royal power within the capital city, with its palace and other buildings from which the various duties and demands of the state could be carried out.

This concentration of buildings next to one another, each with a different function and separated from the city by a strong encircling wall, is characteristic of the royal palace complexes in Samaria. Since detailed descriptions of the various parts of the palace of Solomon are given in 1 Kgs 7.1-12, a similar grouping of the various buildings inside a precinct enclosed by a wall can be assumed to have existed in Jerusalem. Thus a particular form was established for the royal residence in Israel. Even if the royal residence allows recognition of the fact that Canaanite building traditions were taken over, the organization of free-standing

20. Reconstruction by Z. Herzog in *Architecture*, p. 194, Abb. 5.

individual buildings inside the palace precinct was first developed in the period of the monarchy.[21] As a variation on this principle buildings also sometimes bordered on this precinct, as is seen in the case of the acropolis of Lachish (see above, Chapter 5). By contrast, the palaces of the Middle and Later Bronze Ages were closed building complexes, for which the grouping of the rooms around large courts was characteristic. This independent aspect of Israelite palatial architecture as opposed to the Canaanite concept can be demonstrated in a further example.

Khirbet Ṣāliḥ

The hill called *Ramat Rahel* today is situated about 6 km south of Jerusalem. The palace complex dating from the seventh century which has been excavated there (Stratum V A) was destroyed by later buildings constructed on top of it, but the basic layout is still recognizable from the ground plan (fig. 47).[22] It was preceded by an earlier complex dating from the eighth century, but this has largely disappeared and cannot be reconstructed (Stratum V B). The actual palace complex of about 75 × 50 m in area on the plateau of the hill was surrounded by a casemate wall of varying width. The entrance was situated on the eastern side, whereby two casemates formed the gate chambers, and this was adjoined by a narrow secondary entrance in the south. Two large buildings can be identified inside the complex; these stood at right angles to each other, so that a large open court was formed in front of them. The eastern complex seems to have been constructed according to the plan of the courtyard type of building. An underground passage leads from it under the casemate wall out into the open, thus affording the possibility of an unnoticed escape route. The western building is in too bad a condition to enable any certain reconstruction or identification of its function. All the sections of wall that have been preserved are of well-hewn ashlar blocks, and numerous fragments of the building embellishments were found in the building debris; these will be discussed separately. The area surrounding the acropolis was probably enclosed within walls; however, only fragments of these have been excavated in various places. The precinct thus

21. Cf. V. Fritz, 'Paläste während der Bronze- und Eisenzeit in Palästina', *ZDPV* 99 (1983), pp. 1-42.
22. Y. Aharoni, *Excavations at Ramat Rahel. Seasons 1961 and 1962* (1964).

delineated remained devoid of buildings. It is impossible to say whether it was given the particular layout of a garden or park, but the walls clearly indicate where this area belonged.

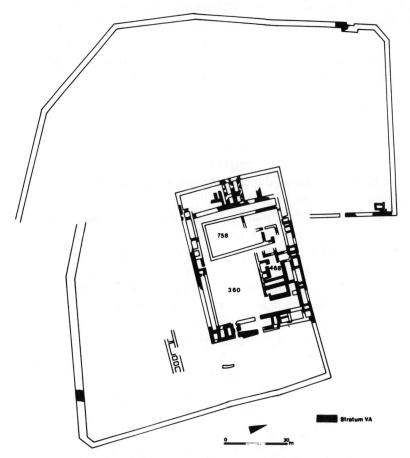

Figure 47. Khirbet Ṣāliḥ. *Palace of Stratum V.*

Pieces of building embellishments have been found in several locations, but only at *Khirbet Ṣāliḥ* do all three elements occur together. These are volute capitals, stepped crenellations and window balustrades with palmette columns. As in other places, the finds here were all made amongst building debris, so that in each case their original position in the building itself has to be conjectured. It can be assumed here that all the worked stones belonged to buildings which, because of their special function, would have been constructed by royal mandate, even though in most cases the location of the individual finds does not permit any final assignment to any one building.

Three complete and seven fragmentary volute capitals were found at *Khirbet Ṣāliḥ* (fig. 48). Other examples are distributed over the whole country and throughout the entire period: one each from Dan and possibly Gezer, two each from Hazor and Jerusalem, four from *Medēbi'* in Transjordan, seven from Samaria and thirteen from Megiddo.[23] The distribution is naturally a reflection of the degree of excavation that has taken place, but it does indicate a clear predominance of finds in places where there is definite evidence of royal building works.

Figure 48. *Volute capital from* Khirbet Ṣāliḥ.

In spite of certain differences in their finish, the capitals always have volutes which curve outwards, and originate from a pointed triangle. Both above and below the volutes there is a leaf, and the empty space between the upper curve of the volute and the triangle is sometimes filled with concentric circles. This is closed off by an abacus in the form of a right angled block on top (fig. 48). Most volute capitals are decorated on one side, and only in three cases is there decoration on both sides. The latter indicates their use on stone pillars, while for the majority a location in a doorway or on top of a pilaster can be assumed. Since the effect of volute capitals would almost have been lost in the doorways,

23. Cf. the list in Y. Shiloh, *The Proto-aeolic Capital and Israelite Ashlar Masonry* (Qedem 11; 1979), with the additions by H. Weippert, 'Ein vergessenes Volutenkapitell aus Jerusalem?', *BN* 26 (1985), pp. 22-26. The supposed capital from Gezer has not yet been located, cf. B. Brandl, 'A Proto-aeolic Capital from Gezer?', *IEJ* 34 (1984), pp. 173-76. Cf. also K. Prag, 'Decorative Architecture in Ammon, Moab and Judah', *Levant* 19 (1987), pp. 121-27.

their use at the end of a pilaster is more probable. Even if pilaster construction has not been discerned as yet in the foundations, this assumption is still justified since the relief-like pillar part of a pilaster can only be
distinguished in the courses of walls that rise above the foundations. The
question of whether the pilaster was situated on the inner or outer walls
must remain open.

The volute capital was widely distributed in the representational art of
the Near East from the third millennium onwards. 'The motif apparently
arose out of a geometric stylization and progressive shortening of the
representation of the palm tree',[24] and was used in various contexts.
Developed volute capitals are only found outside Israel on Cyprus, from
the seventh century onwards. On the evidence of the local and chronological distribution of the pieces found to date, this form of capital could
certainly have been developed in Israel, as has been assumed by
Y. Shiloh. In view of the role played by the Phoenicians in the planning
and execution of Solomon's building works, a Phoenician share in the
transformation of the motif into a building ornament is at least probable.

The stepped crenellations which have been found at Samaria,
Megiddo, and on *Tell Mubārak* as well as on *Khirbet Ṣāliḥ* were without doubt part of the external decoration.[25] Since the palaces as well as
the houses had flat roofs, these crenellations can only have been positioned on the edge of the roof at regular intervals. This ornamental
arrangement serves as an optical relief to the covering of the building.[26]

In contrast to most private houses the palaces had windows (cf.
Judg. 5.28; 2. Sam. 6.16; 2 Kgs 9.30).[27] The shape of these windows can
be deduced from the ivory depicting 'the woman in the window'. The
frame projects inwards in two stages, and underneath the window
opening there is a decorative balustrade of three or four columns with a
garland of leaves, palmette capitals and an abacus. One-piece windows of
this type have been found on Cyprus, but here there were only two
columns in each case under the window opening. On analogy with this

24. Weippert, 'Ein vergessenes Volutenkapitell aus Jerusalem?', p. 446. For
examples see Shiloh, *The Proto-aeolic Capital*, pp. 26-29.
25. Proof in E. Stern, 'The Excavations at Tell Mevorach and the Late Phoenician
Elements in the Architecture of Palestine', *BASOR* 225 (1977), pp. 17-28.
26. As an example cf. the ivory from Nimrud, *ANET*[3], Nr. 131. The meaning of
the motif does not need to be examined here but cf. also R. Barnett, *Catalogue of the
Nimrud Ivories* (1957), pp. 145ff.
27. K. Galling, 'Miscellanea Archaeologica, 1. Steinerne Rahmenfenster', *ZDPV*
83 (1967), pp. 123-25; Shiloh, *The Proto-aeolic Capital*, Pl. 19.

representation several pieces of columns only 36.5 cm high with palmette capitals which were found at *Khirbet Ṣāliḥ* can be identified as the remains of window balustrades.[28] Columns and capitals were finished separately and later joined together by means of pegs; the remains of red colour indicates that the limestone was painted. No trace of the abacus on top has been found. The fragment of a limestone slab with a balustrade in semi-relief from *Khirbet Ṣāliḥ* corroborates this reconstruction; this slab was probably part of a window parapet.[29] The flat, smooth façade of the palace buildings was probably relieved by this form of window. The column type points to north Syrian influences, as have also been shown in the column base with leaf ornament from Dan, the only one of its kind extant to date.[30]

Because of its decoration, the building at *Khirbet Ṣāliḥ* takes on a special significance. In view of the layout Helga Weppert has already drawn attention to the correspondence between the building complex at *Khirbet Ṣāliḥ* and the acropolis at Samaria.[31] Since such a resemblance cannot be ignored, this complex can also be termed a royal residence, even if another Davidic palace outside Jerusalem is not mentioned in the Books of the Kings. The existence side by side of two palaces is attested in the northern kingdom. As well as at Samaria, the kings of Israel also resided in a palace at Jesreel, which was built by Ahab (1 Kgs 21.1). This residence was referred to by several names (cf. 1 Kgs 21.1-16; 2 Kgs 9.16-10.11).[32] Thus the residence at *Khirbet Ṣāliḥ* could easily have been the summer residence of the kings of Judah, since its function as an administrative seat is excluded because of its immediate proximity to the capital. Finally, its particular architectural embellishments also indicate that the complex had a special function.

28. Illustrated in Shiloh, *The Proto-aeolic Capital*, Pl. 14.3.

29. Shiloh, *The Proto-aeolic Capital*, Pl. 14.2.

30. A. Biran (Antike Welt 15/1; 1984), p. 47, Abb. 19. Cf. also B. Wesenberg, *Kapitelle und Basen* (1971).

31. Weippert, 'Ein vergessenes Volutenkapitell aus Jerusalem?', p. 599.

32. Cf. H.G.M. Williamson, 'Jezreel in the Biblical Texts', *Tel Aviv* 18 (1991), pp. 72-92.

Chapter 7

BUILDING AND DWELLING

In Hebrew, the city wall (*ḥômāh*) is differentiated from the wall of a building (*qîr*). Both were constructed in the same way; however, the width of the walls varied according to function. Stone and mud bricks served as building materials, and sometimes wooden beams were used as a stabilizing element. The stones were either simply collected (field stones) or extracted by quarrying and roughly hewn (quarry stones). The use of stones with hewn right-angled corners which could then be laid down accurately was limited to public buildings and fortifications (ashlar stones); here, the occasional masons' marks indicate that the stones were produced in the quarries. The mud bricks were manufactured in a wooden mould from a mixture of mud, chopped straw and water, and were air-dried. Mortar was not used in construction, but in the case of walls made of quarry stones the interstices between the larger stones were filled with smaller ones; mud-brick walls were covered with a layer of lime plaster.

The use of the two main building materials fluctuated strongly according to the region.[1] As a rule, the foundations were built of stones to a height of 60–80 cm above the floor level, in order to protect the wall against spray from water. The rest of the wall was then built using mud bricks. In the mountains, the whole of the ground floor was built of stone, and mud bricks were only used for the upper floor. By contrast, brick-built structures predominated in the coastal plain, and occasionally the foundations consisted of mud brick or a compressed layer of the sandy floor which exists there. The width of the walls in the case of domestic architecture fluctuated between 60 and 80 cm, with both sides of the wall carefully positioned and only the space between them filled in.

1. On the building materials and forms of construction cf. G.R.H. Wright, *Ancient Building in South Syria and Palestine* (1985), pp. 337-472.

The city walls exhibit certain variations in construction. Apart from the solid wall there is the casemate wall in use; both of these can have forward or backward projecting buttresses and jutting towers. The various building techniques employed in the fortifications were used alongside each other during the whole period of the monarchy; at any rate, no particular regional or chronological distribution has been discerned to date. The solid wall has an average width of 4–5 m, but it can reach 9 m as in Lachish Stratum II or up to 10 m as in Kinneret Stratum V. The width is not only explained by the intention to provide adequate resistance at times of attack, as well as a certain stability, but also by the need to be able to walk along the top of the wall. To what degree the wall was finished with a rampart and defensive breastwork is unknown, but the existence of both elements is to be assumed. Because of the strong internal pressure exerted by the filling inside the wall, support was sometimes given by means of a retaining wall, and the outer wall occasionally found at sites also constituted a further security measure. The frequent insets and outsets as well as the relatively rare towers increased the defensibility, since they allowed the enemy to be fired upon from a sideways direction. The concept which lay behind the building method employed for walls was thus determined by constructional as well as defensive considerations. The solid wall was in use as an urban fortification from the Early Bronze Age onwards.

The casemate wall had the advantage that, since the crest of the wall had a uniform thickness, fewer building materials were necessary and by the same token the pressure exerted by the building materials against the outer edge was reduced. In addition the space saved could be utilized. Thus in numerous cities the houses were constructed against the external wall in such a way that the casemate formed the back room of the private house (cf. fig. 40). Normally the external wall had a thickness of 1.5 to 1.6 m, so that with a distance of 1.5 to 2.5 m between the two the wall had a total width of 4–5 m.[2] Projecting and recessed buttresses, as well as towers, are rare with this form. The origin of the casemate style of building has not yet been established; it was not used in the Canaanite city during the Late Bronze Age. Casemates are only known from the Hittite capital Hattuša-Bogazköy in the period before 1200 BC. Thus the Iron Age casemate walls in the area of northern Syria, at

2.   Cf. the list in N.L. Lapp, 'Casemate Walls in Palestine and the Late Iron II Casemate at Tell el-Ful (Gibeah)', *BASOR* 223 (1976), pp. 25-42.

Carchemish and Zincirli, are probably attributable to Hittite influences.[3] Whether the casemate building form was taken over from north Syrian building tradition lies beyond our knowledge. At any rate, the free-standing casemate walls in Hazor Stratum X and on *Tell Qemūn* Stratum XI belong to the tenth century;[4] thus they could be evidence of a foreign influence that is elsewhere visible in the early period of the monarchy, without the question of how they passed into the tradition of the country being solvable at present. Even if the casemate can be included among domestic building forms, its origin can by no means be adduced from the settlement form of the Early Iron Age.[5]

As a rule, entrance to the city is through a single gate, and only in the capital cities can the existence of several gates be reckoned with, on account of the physical extent of the city. This opening in the city wall was especially secured by a gatehouse, in view of its vulnerability at times of attack; such a gatehouse could in turn also be given further protection through additional constructional measures. Various gate complexes can be distinguished on typological grounds: there are gates with one, two, or three chambers each on both sides of the gateway passage (fig. 49).[6] All three types were in use during the whole of the Iron Age II, whereby the actual gate construction was normally situated inside the city. However, as at Beth-Shean Stratum V, it could also project out of the city wall. Access was at a right angle to the wall, and occasionally the gate was placed parallel to the city wall, as at Dan and Mizpa.

---

3. Cf. K. Bittel, *Die Hethiter* (1976), p. 112, Abb. 104; R. Naumann, *Architektur Kleinasiens* (2nd edn, 1971), pp. 309-10.

4. Cf. Yadin, *Hazor*, pp. 136-37; A. Ben-Tor, Y. Portugali and M. Avissar, 'The Third and Fourth Seasons of Excavations at Tel Yoqne'am, 1979 and 1981', *IEJ* 33 (1983), pp. 30-54, Pl. 2.4.6. Because of the unclear nature of the findings Ashdod Stratum X A has not been taken into consideration here.

5. As opposed to Y. Shiloh, 'Elements in the Development of Town Planning in the Israelite City', *IEJ* 28 (1978), pp. 36-51.

6. A compilation and discussion of the gates in Z. Herzog, *Das Stadttor in Israel und in den Nachbarländern* (1986). For the gate at Megiddo now cf. D. Ussishkin, 'Was the "Solomonic" City Gate at Megiddo Built by King Solomon?', *BASOR* 239 (1980), pp. 1-18; on the gate at Kinneret cf. V. Fritz, *Tel Aviv* 20 (1993), p. 199, fig. 6 and for the gate in Jezreel cf. D. Ussishkin and J. Woodhead, 'Excavations at Tel Jezreel 1992–1993: Second 'Preliminary Report', *Levant* 24 (1994), pp. 1-48, fig. 5.

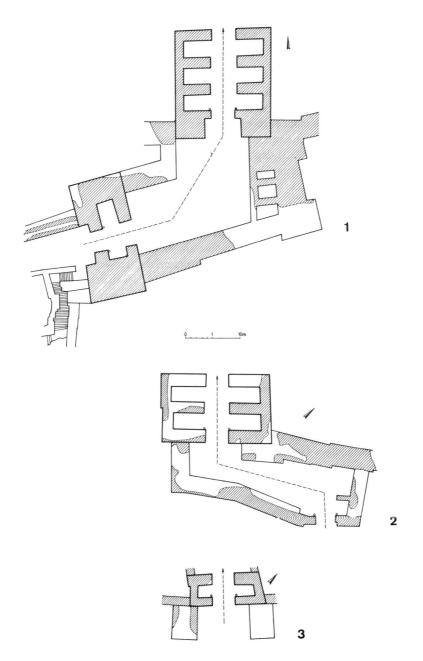

Figure 49. *Gates of the Iron Age II: 1. Six chamber gate (Megiddo Stratum IV B).*
*2. Four chamber gate (*Tell es-Seba') *Stratum V.*
*3. Two chamber gate (*Tell Beit Mirsim *Stratum A).*

As in Hazor Stratum X and on *Tell Beit Mirsim* Stratum A (fig. 49.3) the gate could be equipped with projecting towers, which permitted a better defence of the square in front of it. A preliminary gate was built in front of the main gate for purposes of further security in Megiddo Stratum IV B (fig. 49.1), in Lachish Strata III and II, and on *Tell es-Seba'* Stratum V (fig 49.2). The pathway up to the gate ran parallel to the wall as far as possible, so that attackers could be fired upon from the sides and had to make a turn of ninety degrees in front of the gate. The two halves of the door in the gateway were closed at night. The pathway led into the centre of the city, as a rule to a small square. In addition to its military function, which was that of defending the access to the city, the gate also had a civilian one, in that its rooms provided a certain place where people could meet for political consultations or judgments could take place (cf. Deut. 21.19; Amos 5.12; Zech. 8.16). However, the sparse finds of cultic objects do not permit recognition of cultic practice in the area of the gate.

In its various forms, the gateway construction was already in use in the second millennium. With the exception of the gate with three chambers on each side of the gateway path, the chambered gate was widely distributed in Canaan as well as in Syria and Anatolia.[7] As an independent building structure the chambered gate thus already developed in the Canaanite culture and was taken over in Israel, together with other elements designed for the fortification of the newly-founded cities.

On grounds of access, the gate was mostly situated at the lowest point of the city. This served also for purposes of drainage, since most of the roads ended at the gate. There was no further planning behind the system of streets, which can rather be described as twisted alleys between the rows of houses. Certain principles of planning are only recognizable in the cities with a military or administrative function; such principles have resulted in the establishment of a 'ring road' or street parallel to the city wall, and in the construction of regular blocks of houses (cf. fig. 40). On *Tell es-Seba'* a system of drainage canals was planned and laid out along with the network of streets. This drainage system was below street level and led out through the gate into the open. It is unknown whether these drains also collected waste water in

---

7.   The other types of gates of the Middle and Late Bronze Age need not be gone into here, cf. fig. 10. Of particular interest is the gate completely preserved under later deposits at Dan, dating from the Middle Bronze Age. Cf. A. Biran, 'The Triple-arched Gate of Laish at Tel Dan', *IEJ* 34 (1984), pp. 1-19.

addition to rainwater. The remains of such channels were also found at Megiddo, Gezer and Lachish.

Inside the city, the houses were built close together, their walls abutting each other. Despite the irregularity in the form of construction the three- and four-room house predominates; this was already developed during the Early Iron Age and can be designated as the ancient Israelite farm-house (cf. above, Chapter 4). It is an attestation of cultural and economic continuity; even in the new form of settlement the old patterns of life and work were preserved. This type of courtyard house is found in monotonous rows along the casemate wall (cf. figs. 39, 40); it is also suited to the construction of residential blocks (cf. fig. 44).

The way in which the four-room house and its smaller variant the three-room house were used is apparent from the layout.[8] The central space, with the entrance generally leading into it, is recognizable as a court.[9] Accordingly it was not roofed over and its floor was made of ash mixed with compressed clay soil. Since the court did not incorporate any built-in drainage, the floor had to be constructed in such a way that the rainwater could seep away effectively into it.[10] The rooms on the long sides of the court were often completely or partly separated from it by stone pillars, and mostly paved with small stones. Their exact function cannot definitely be ascertained, but they most likely served a domestic purpose in view of the fact that they were constructed so as to afford adequate light and ventilation. The room at the back extended along the whole width of the house but could also be divided into two units by a wall in the middle; light and ventilation were provided only through the doorway. This room is probably to be designated as the actual living room, which served simultaneously as a bedroom. Except on days when it rained, life was generally carried on in the courtyard. A stairway which was occasionally located near the entrance led up to the roof, which was used for drying and storing agricultural produce and also as a place to sleep. Although there is no actual proof to support the hypothesis, it can be reckoned that part of the roof was probably also

8. Cf. H.K. Beebe, 'Ancient Palestinian Dwellings', *BA* 31 (1968), pp. 38-58.

9. The identification of the central space as a court has recently been contested, cf. F. Braemer, *L'architecture domestique du Levant à l'âge du fer* (1982). In opposition to this it should be maintained, along with E. Heinrich, 'Haus', *RLA* IV, pp. 176-220, that the court was an integral component of this building type.

10. Cf. here the examination in Y. Itzhaki and M. Shinar, '"Dust and Ashes" as Floor Stabilizers in Iron Age Beer-sheba', in Y. Aharoni (ed.), *Beer-sheba*, I (1973), pp. 18-22.

built upon, so that the existence of additional rooms on the upper floor can be assumed. The roofs were flat and supported by beams placed on top of the walls or stone pillars. The simple construction demanded frequent repairs to the roof, which was given a simple earth or mud covering after the rainy period.

Apart from small variations in the way in which the building was carried out, this normal Israelite form of house exhibits an astonishing rigidity in concept, as well as a wide distribution. The overall minimal fluctuations in size point to a certain social equality among the members of a rural population. Only in the case of the house next to the gate can a function connected with the defence of the city be postulated.

A constructional form related to that of the private house is represented by the pillar-house, which is found as a single building in Hazor Stratum VIII as well as in rows at Megiddo Stratum IV A, Kinneret Stratum II and on *Tell es-Seba'* Stratum II (cf. figs. 26, 29, 31, 40). The division of a long house by two rows of stone pillars into three parallel units is characteristic.[11] The middle part was mostly a little wider than the other two and probably not roofed over, a fact indicated by the floor of stamped earth. Accordingly it must have served as a courtyard, while the side rooms were roofed over and had paved floors. The size and number of the buildings exclude the possibility that they were put to private use; thus an official function is to be assumed. The numerous vessels, which were mainly found in the side rooms, make it most likely that the latter were used for habitation; thus the possibility that they were used as stables or as storerooms is excluded.[12] A designation as a market hall is to be rejected, since the inhabitants of the city were self-supporting farmers.[13] This complex is more likely to have been a barracks for the accommodation of soldiers of the professional army. The troops stationed here were less concerned with the defence of the city—this was an obligation which fell to the inhabitants—but rather

11. Cf. here Pritchard, 'Megiddo Stables', in *Archaeology in the Twentieth Century*, pp. 268-76; V. Fritz, 'Bestimmung und Herkunft des Pfeilerhauses in Israel', *ZDPV* 93 (1977), pp. 30-45.

12. Contra Z. Herzog, 'The Storehouses', in Y. Aharoni (ed.), *Beer-sheba*, I (1973), pp. 23-30; Y. Yadin, 'The Megiddo Stables', in *Magnalia Dei—The Mighty Acts of God* (1976), pp. 249-52; J.S. Holladay, 'The Stables of Ancient Israel', in *The Archaeology of Jordan and Other Studies* (ed. L.T. Geraty and L.G. Herr; 1986), pp. 103-65.

13. As opposed to L.G. Herr, 'Tripartite Pillared Buildings and the Market Place in Iron Age Palestine', *BASOR* 272 (1988), pp. 47-67.

with the military security of the country and its borders. The pottery found in the pillar-houses comprised the total repertoire[14] and thus permits the assumption that the soldiers themselves cooked the rations which had been apportioned to them.

It is not only on grounds of size that the palaces are to be differentiated from the private houses and thus occupy a particular position; the palace was not only lavishly built as befitted the residence of the king or his official representative, but as the seat of government it incorporated rooms in which official business and the administration of the kingdom were carried on. The palace built by Solomon in Jerusalem consisted—apart from the temple—of at least five buildings which are named in 1 Kgs 7.1-12, without the description being sufficient to enable a reconstruction. In addition, the presence of other annexed buildings for the royal household is to be assumed. The whole complex was surrounded by a wall and formed the city acropolis which, in the position occupied by the temple square today, towered up over the city to the south of it. That substantial parts of the palace have been preserved cannot be expected, since this whole precinct was thoroughly cleared for the radical reconstruction of the temple at the time of Herod.

The palaces of Samaria and *Khirbet Ṣāliḥ* also present an incomplete picture because of their bad state of preservation (cf. above, Chapter 6 and figs. 46, 47). Within a precinct enclosed by a wall, several buildings served various functions; the actual residence of the king was the largest of all these buildings. As far as their layout is concerned, the palatial buildings seem to have had their roots in the Canaanite building tradition of the courtyard house. There is nothing left of the interior built structures of the residential palaces, but the few pieces of building embellishments which have been preserved show that they must have differed radically from those of the normal private house. Not only the size and number of the rooms distinguish the palace from the private house, but the way in which they were constructed indicates a certain affluence. The power of the king was to be reflected in the magnificence of his buildings, although the manifestation of this splendour remained within the limits posed by the small states of Israel and Judah.

In addition to the royal palaces and residences there were also palaces in the administrative and military centres, which can be designated as the places of residence of the king's local representative. It is not known to

14. Cf. Aharoni (ed.) *Beer-sheba*, I (1973), Pl. 57-63; V. Fritz, *Kinneret* (1990), Pl. 89-93.

what degree they were used by the king on journeys or campaigns. The occurrence of double palaces in Lachish Strata IV and III could be due to the fact that a part was reserved for the king (cf. fig. 36); the location of the two palaces 1723 and 6000 in Megiddo Stratum V A could also reflect the practice of holding one in readiness (cf. fig. 30). A hallmark of these palaces in Megiddo is the arrangement of the rooms around an open courtyard, which also points to an architectural history connected with the Canaanite courtyard house. The palace at Lachish cannot be assigned to a category as yet because of its very bad state of preservation.

During the course of the period of the monarchy an individual type of palatial residence was developed for royal representatives; this is evidenced by the so-called citadel in Hazor Strata VIII–V and by building 338 in Megiddo Stratum IV B (cf. figs. 27, 31). Although the function of the individual groups of rooms is unknown, both the absence of a courtyard and the addition of a square tower are conspicuous. The rooms are arranged in such a way that one row of rooms is set at an oblique angle to the rooms arranged along the length of the building.[15]

Towards the end of the eighth century a new type of palace is found, the introduction of which is directly connected with the supremacy of the Assyrians in the southern Levant starting with the time of Tiglath-Pileser III.[16] A hallmark of this new constructional form is the extraordinarily large courtyard in the centre and the careful planning of the residential quarter with its wide rooms, which as a rule was situated in the south. Examples of these palaces are building 3002 in Hazor Stratum III,[17] building 737 in Kinneret[18] and buildings 1052 and 1369 in Megiddo Stratum III (cf. fig. 32).[19] The plan of these palaces follows the tradition of the Babylonian courtyard house,[20] thus demonstrating the

15. The construction inside the oldest fortification on *Tell el-Helēfe* at the southern end of the Arabah is the same type of building, cf. G.D. Pratico, 'Nelson Glueck's 1938–40 Excavations at Tell el-Kheleifeh: A Reappraisal', *BASOR* 259 (1985), pp. 1-32, fig. 5.

16. Cf. V. Fritz, 'Die Paläste während der assyrischen, babylonischen und persischen Vorherrschaft in Palästina', *MDOG* 111 (1979), pp. 63-74.

17. Cf. Yadin, *Hazor*, pp. 191-94.

18. Cf. Fritz, *Kinneret*, pp. 99-102.

19. The so-called Residency of Lachish has to be dated to the Persian period, in contrast to Y. Aharoni, *Investigations at Lachish* (1975), pp. 33-40. Cf. D. Ussishkin, 'The Destruction of Lachish by Sennacherib and the Dating of the Royal Judean Storage Jars', *Tel Aviv* 4 (1977), [28-60] 36-39.

20. Cf. O. Reuther, 'Das babylonische Wohnhaus', *MDOG* 64 (1926), pp. 3-32.

acquisition of a building tradition from southern Mesopotamia. This new form of palace is first encountered in the period of the Assyrian hegemony, but continues during the periods of the Babylonian and Persian administration. The historical connections lead to the assumption that these buildings with a central courtyard served the governors of the respective great powers, and are thus to be described as administrative centres in the provinces.

In contrast to the Canaanite period, cultic architecture is apparently not a constitutive element of the ancient Israelite city. Thus as yet no temple complexes have been discovered in the extensively excavated sites of Megiddo, Mizpa and Lachish. It does seem, however, that at least individual sanctuaries existed in the cities. This is not only attested by texts such as 1 Kgs 12.25-30 or Amos 4.4f., in which the construction of temples in Dan, Bel-El and Gilgal is mentioned or presupposed.[21] The stones from an altar secondarily built into a wall in Stratum II on *Tell es-Seba'* prove that local cultic places existed before 700.[22] After 700 the picture changed radically, when the centralization of cultic practices in the temple at Jerusalem, as defined in Deuteronomy 12, was carried through as a political measure.[23] It can thus be assumed for the period before 700 that temples for the veneration of Yahweh and the bringing of offerings existed in numerous cities. Only the temple at Jerusalem and the temple at Arad are well-known at present, the former on the basis of the description in 1 Kings 6 and the latter as a result of archaeological excavation.

The information in 1 Kgs 6.1-12 permits the assumption that the temple of Solomon in Jerusalem was constructed as a long-room temple with a vestibule hall (fig. 50).[24] Its plan corresponds to the so-called

21. On the village sanctuaries cf. Th. Oestreicher, *Reichstempel und Ortsheiligtümer in Israel* (1930). None of the temples mentioned in the Bible have yet been discovered.

22. Cf. Y. Aharoni, 'The Horned Altar of Beer-sheba', *BA* 37 (1974), pp. 2-6.

23. For the significance of the centralization of cultic practice in Jerusalem cf. V. Maag, 'Erwägungen zur deuteronomischen Kultzentralisation', in *Kultur, Kulturkontakt und Religion* (1980), pp. 90-98; E. Nicholson, 'The Centralisation of the Cult in Deuteronomy', *VT* 13 (1963), pp. 380-89; M. Weinfeld, 'Cult Centralisation in Israel in the Light of a Neo-Babylonian Analogy', *JNES* 23 (1964), pp. 202-12.

24. Cf. Th. A. Busink, *Der Tempel von Jerusalem von Salomo bis Herodes I. Der Tempel Salomos* (1970); V. Fritz, 'Der Tempel Salomos im Licht der neueren Forschung', *MDOG* 112 (1980), pp. 53-68. The annexe described in 1 Kgs 6.6-10 is both a literary and constructional embellishment. Cf. K. Rupprecht, 'Nachrichten

north Syrian type of temple, which was already well established during
the second millennium in Syria and was taken over from there by the
Canaanites; it can originally be traced back to the older building form of
the Megaron.[25] The takeover of this form of building, which was alien to
Israel, could have been the result of Canaanite or Phoenician agency.
Foreign elements are also indicated by the rich fittings and furnishings,
which are comprehensively described in 1 Kgs 6.14-36. They included a
wooden shrine, the Holy of Holies, and wooden panelling with figurative
representations. The objects necessary for cultic practices were mostly of
bronze, and their manufacture by Phoenician craftsman is expressly
mentioned in 1 Kgs 7.13-47. Founded as a state sanctuary, the temple at

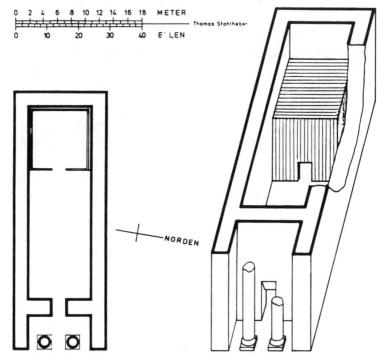

Figure 50. *Reconstruction of the temple in Jerusalem built by Solomon.*

von Erweiterung und Renovierung des Tempels in 1 Kings 6', *ZDPV* 88 (1972),
pp. 38-52.

    25. The best parallel is offered by the temple of the eighth century on *Tell
Ta'yīnāt* in the valley of the Orontes, cf. R.C. Haines, *Excavations in the Plain of
Antioch*, II (1971), pp. 53-55, Pl. 80-83.

Jerusalem subsequently acquired a predominant importance as the only legitimate place for the practice of the Yahweh cult.[26] Thus the temple at Jerusalem not only constituted the centre of the capital, but it was also the centre of worship in Judah. However, this claim could never quite be realized, as is shown by the new foundation of temples in different places down into Hellenistic times.[27] From the architectural point of view the temple of Solomon was a foreign element within the Israelite city; its particular form was appropriate to its special significance, as can be seen earlier in Canaanite temple architecture (cf. figs. 5–7).

In addition there also existed a form of cultic architecture orientated towards domestic architecture in Israel. The only Israelite temple from the period of the monarchy known to date has been uncovered in the fortress of Arad, which was situated in the northern Negev.[28] The temple was located in the north-west of the fortress and was in use during Strata XI-VIII from the tenth to the eighth century.[29] The whole complex had a west-east orientation and consisted of a wide-room with a niche, a court and an additional room on the long side of the court (fig. 51). There was a stone-built altar in the courtyard, which was moved from its original position in the middle to the edge by later building measures. The recess opposite the entrance was raised and only accessible via a small flight of three steps; only two stelae and two incense-altars remain of the internal structures (fig. 52). No alterations were made to the cultic room during the period of its use until the end of the eighth century, while various building modifications were undertaken in the courtyard.

In contrast to the Temple of Jerusalem the cultic building at Arad is of the wide-room type, and measures 20 × 6 cubits internally. Although individual examples of wide-room temples lasted down until 1500 BC, it is unlikely that this building form was taken over from the environment,

26. Cf. G. Westphal, *Jahwes Wohnstätten* (BZAW 15; 1908); M. Metzger, 'Himmlische und irdische Wohnstatt Jahwes', *UF* 2 (1970), pp. 139-58.
27. Cf. the summary in Fritz, *Tempel und Zelt*, pp. 76-87. The Hellenistic building *Qaṣr el-'Abd* in *'Arāq el-Emīr* was recently and decisively identified as a palace.
28. On the excavations cf. Y. Aharoni, 'Arad: Its Inscriptions and Temple', *BA* 31 (1968), pp. 2-32; Z. Herzog, M. Aharoni, A.F. Rainey, Sh. Moshkovitz, 'The Israelite Fortress at Arad', *BASOR* 254 (1984), pp. 1-34.
29. As only preliminary reports have been issued up till now, the stratigraphical problems cannot be further discussed; cf. D. Ussishkin, 'The Date of the Judaean Shrine at Arad', *IEJ* 38 (1988), pp. 142-57.

since in the Canaanite culture the wide-room type of temple was replaced by the long-room temple during the second millennium.[30]

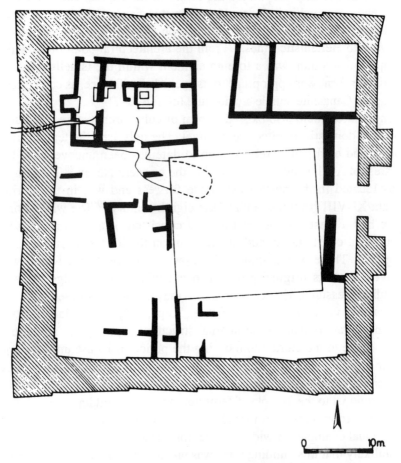

Figure 51. *Arad. The fortress with the temple in Stratum X.*

However the simple wide-room type exhibits a connection with Israelite building tradition, inasmuch as the broadroom house is found among the forms of domestic architecture during the Early Iron Age (cf. Chapter 4). Thus it can most likely be assumed that the temple of Arad has its

30. On Canaanite architecture cf. G.R.H. Wright, 'Pre-Israelite Temples in the Land of Canaan', *PEQ* 103 (1971), pp. 17-32; I. Dunayevsky and A. Kempinski, 'The Megiddo Temples', *ZDPV* 89 (1973), pp. 161-87; M. Ottoson, *Temples and Cult Places in Palestine* (1980); G.R.H. Wright, *Ancient Building in South Syria and Palestine* (1985), pp. 215-47.

Figure 52. *Arad. The niche of the temple in Stratum X.*

roots in the ancient Israelite tradition of building.[31] To house cultic objects, the wide-room was extended with a recess to the back of it. The broad-room temple with niche and court in front thus probably developed as an Israelite form of temple from the domestic house form and was in use down into Hellenistic times, as is demonstrated by

31. The identification as 'Kulthöhe' by P. Welten in 'Kulthöhe und Jahwetempel', *ZDPV* 88 (1972), pp. 19-37 is not justified in view of the building form.

The City in Ancient Israel

examples at Lachish and on *Tell es-Seba'*.[32] As opposed to the temple at Jerusalem, the temple at Arad created a special house for the presence of Yahweh and for his veneration.

32. Cf. Y. Aharoni, *Investigations at Lachish* (1975), pp. 3-11; *idem, Tel Aviv* 2 (1975), pp. 163-65.

Chapter 8

THE WATER SUPPLY

The defence of a city was dependent not only upon the strength and condition of the fortifications, but also on the provisioning of its inhabitants. Only with an adequate stock of foodstuffs and a water supply was a city able to hold out during siege, which could sometimes last for years (cf. 2 Kgs 17.5). Thus the safeguard of an assured water supply for man and beast made special measures necessary; either large water-storage facilities for the collection of rainwater or a secret access to a spring had to be provided, which could also be used without problem at times of siege. To date, large rainwater collection reservoirs hewn in the rock have only been found in the fortress of Arad.[1] There natural holes in the rock were made use of when these storage facilities were constructed, and they were filled via a covered canal in the west, the opening of which was situated outside the fortress. The structures were filled up during the rainy period, when animals were used to transport water from a cistern in the vicinity. This laborious supply method was necessary because there was no water source in the vicinity of Arad. In view of the considerable effort involved, this solution only seems to have been used in cases when there was no access to a spring or ground water itself.

The safeguarding of the access to a place where there was a continuous flow of water from within the city could only be achieved via deep shafts and long tunnels. The excavation of such passages represented a significant achievement and necessitated a high degree of technical knowledge. The carrying out of such measures was also dependent upon the existence of suitable tools, and was first realized with the advent of the iron pick, after the hardening of iron by the appropriate forging technique had been developed at the beginning of the Iron Age. The oldest example of such a pick comes from the twelfth century and is

1.   Cf. the plan of Arad Stratum X in *BASOR* 254 (1984), p. 10, Fig. 10 = Fig. 51. This system seems to have been in use until the end of the Iron Age fortress.

made of iron hardened to steel;[2] numerous other examples are known from Iron Age II.[3] The innovation of the hewing out of tunnels and shafts, in order to secure the water supply in case of siege, seems first to have been introduced with the development of iron tools;[4] at any rate such installations have not been discovered to date in the Canaanite cities. Even though such hidden passages to vital water supplies from within the city existed in the Mycenaean world,[5] such complicated systems were apparently unknown in Canaan.[6] Thus they must count as an innovation of the period of the monarchy, and one which apart from an enormous expenditure of labour also demanded great dexterity on the part of the workers and technical know-how. Three different solutions to the problems posed may be observed:

1. The access to the ground water supply was inside the city.
2. The spring situated outside the city walls was reached by a hidden passage from the city.
3. Water from a spring outside the city was brought inside the city by a system of subterranean channels.

The first solution was employed at Gibeon, Gezer and Hazor, and also the purpose of the unfinished shaft at Lachish was to reach ground water.[7] A round shaft with a diameter of 10 m was hewn out of the rock at Gibeon, with a spiral shaped flight of hewn steps in its wall that ended in an underground reservoir used to collect ground water

2.   D. Davis, R. Maddin, J.D. Muhly and T. Stech, 'A Steel Pick from Mt. Adir in Palestine', *JNES* 44 (1985), pp. 41-51.

3.   J. Briend and J.B. Humbert, *Tell Keisan (1971–6)* (1980), Pl. 99.1; C.C. McCown, *Tell en Nasbeh*, I (1947), Pl. 96: 17; J.W. Crowfoot, G.M. Crowfoot and K.M. Kenyon, *The Objects from Samaria* (1957), Fig. 113: 8; Y. Shiloh, *BA* 44 (1981), p. 168.

4.   Cf. here T.A. Wertime and J.D. Muhly (ed.), *The Coming of the Age of Iron* (1980).

5.   Cf. with the examples in Mycenae and Tiryns, U. Jantzen, *Führer durch Tiryns* (1975).

6.   The connection between the system of shafts and tunnels and the Early Bronze Age city on *Hirbet ez-Zeraqōn* has by no means been proved; the technical details of these passages in the rock point rather to the dating of the complex to Hellenistic or Roman times.

7.   The shaft with stepped entrance cut into *Tell es-Seba'* was certainly also intended to reach ground water, but it has not been completely uncovered, and can thus be left out of consideration here.

(fig. 53.4).[8] The difference in levels of 25 m between the city and the water-table was thus overcome by means of a flight of 172 steps. The exact dating of this structure is impossible, but it seems to be later than the hidden entrance to the spring.

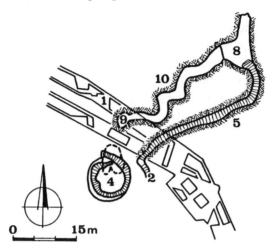

Figure 53. *Gibeon. The water system: 1. City wall. 2. Steps. 4 Shaft with staircase. 5. Passage with steps. 8. Basin. 9. Spring. 10. Tunnel.*

The water supply of Gezer, situated on the southern edge of the city, consists of a passage with a stairway leading downwards and continues over a distance of almost 50 m to a reservoir more than 40 m in length, which was hewn in the rock for the collection of rainwater.[9] This passage was reached via a short stairway at a right angle to it. An exact dating is not possible.

At Hazor, the water supply system was located on the south-eastern edge of the city; when it was constructed, the settlement deposits of the Bronze Age first had to be cut through and a landslide prevented by means of supporting walls (fig. 54).[10] After the bedrock was reached a four-cornered shaft 19 m in depth was excavated, along the side of which there was a wide stairway. On the floor of the shaft the stairway led into a 25 m long tunnel, which after 35 steps ended 10 m lower in a

8. J. Pritchard, *Gibeon, Where the Sun Stood Still* (1962), pp. 53-78.
9. W.G. Dever in 'The Water Systems at Hazor und Gezer', *BA* 32 (1969), pp. 71-78, tried to date the system at Gezer to the Late Bronze Age, but the evidence is undecisive; thus its dating to the Iron Age is a greater probability.
10. Yadin, *Hazor*, pp. 172-78.

collection reservoir for ground water. In all, a difference in height of more than 30 m had to be overcome. The width of the steps leads to the supposition that mules were used for the transport of water. This structure was most probably built in Stratum VIII during the ninth century.

The use of a hidden access to the spring situated outside the city is found at Megiddo and on *Tell es-Sa'idīyeh*, and also in altered form at Gibeon. In the case of Megiddo, at first a four-cornered shaft was sunk on the western edge of the city, and steps hewn out of its walls (fig. 55).[11]

Above the rock the shaft was surrounded by walls, as at Hazor, in order to secure the successive settlement levels and prevent them from causing a landslide; the shaft was accessible via a stairway running in a straight line from the city. Another retaining wall surrounded and secured the whole area. From the shaft, the stairway continued into a passage about 10 m below the solid rock, in order to reach the foot of a tunnel about 60 m long, which ran under the city wall and ended at a small reservoir of spring water. Making use of natural hollows in the rock, ascent out into the open was achieved via a stairway; at time of danger this could be camouflaged. On the basis of further investigation, the whole installation can be assigned to Stratum IV A, and thus dated to the ninth century.[12]

Given the geological nature of the site, a completely different solution for this structure was employed on *Tell es-Sa'idīyeh*.[13] Since the Iron Age city was built upon the settlement levels of the Bronze Age, neither a shaft nor a tunnel could be constructed. Instead a stairway led down on the steep northern slope of the hill which was 2–2.5 m in width and subdivided by a mud-brick wall in the middle so that it could be hidden under a roof and could not be seen from the outside. Access to this stairway was probably by means of a postern in the wall and it ended at the foot of the cliff on a ledge, from which a very steep flight of steps turned away at a right angle towards the east. The latter led to a reservoir, in which the ground water was collected and which in addition fed a spring with water by means of a pipe. A connection was established between the construction of this installation and Stratum XII, thus dating

11. R.S. Lamon, *Megiddo Water System* (1935).
12. Yadin, *Hazor*, pp. 161-64.
13. J.B. Pritchard, *Tell es Sa'idiyeh. Excavations on the Tell 1964–66* (1985), pp. 57-59; R.L. Miller, 'The Water System', *Levant* 20 (1988), pp. 84-89.

it to the twelfth century, but the system also seems to have been in use during the rest of the Iron Age.[14]

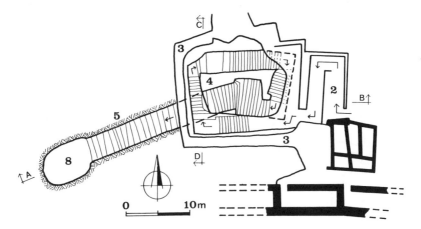

Figure 54. *Hazor. The water system: 2. Entryway. 3. Retaining wall. 4. Shaft with staircase. 5. Passage with steps. 8. Basin (groundwater).*

There is a second water supply system situated immediately next to the shaft at Gibeon, already mentioned above, on the north-western edge of the city (fig. 53).[15] The position of the two systems side by side can probably be explained by the fact that the older of the two was not considered sufficient; the round shaft is probably of later date. At any rate, the position of the spring must have been known at the time of its construction, since it was located immediately to the south of it. Even if the spring was not reached by the shaft, the latter is still an indication of the abundance of water in this place. As the city wall of the Iron Age ran directly over the spring, the latter could not be reached directly by the second system. A passageway with a flight of 93 steps led beneath the city wall through the rock to a subterranean reservoir. The water from the spring was channelled into this via a tunnel which makes several twists and turns as a result of various corrections made during its construction. The reservoir was also accessible from the outside via an opening, which at time of danger could easily be closed off. This system

14. J.N. Tubb, *Levant* 20, 1988, p. 46. The twelfth century date assigned to Stratum XII seems, on the ceramic evidence, to be too high. An exact chronological classification is thus not possible at present.

15. Pritchard, *Gibeon*, pp. 53-78.

cannot be dated exactly, but was constructed at the beginning or during
the course of the period of the monarchy; it is probably older than the
shaft in the city,[16] since it makes use of the covered spring whose existence was known of at the time the city wall was constructed.

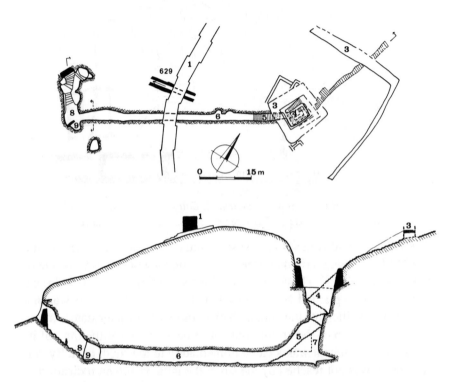

Figure 55. *Megiddo. The water system: 1. City wall. 3. Retaining walls.*
4. Shaft with staircase. 5. Passage with steps. 6. Tunnel. 8. Basin. 9. Spring.

The third variant in the method of water supply—the subterranean
channelling of spring water into the city—has until now only been recognized in Jerusalem.[17] There were three different systems here in the
Iron Age,[18] which were built one after the other but probably all used at
the same time (fig. 56):

16. The argument of Pritchard, *Gibeon*, p. 71, that the layout of the passage presupposes the existence of the shaft, since it ends in a right-angled bend, is not valid.

17. On the history of construction and settlement at Jerusalem cf. H. Weippert,
Palästina in vorhellenistischer Zeit (1988), pp. 451-76 and 587-614.

18. The best summary with a bibliography of the older literature is to be found in
R. Wenning and E. Zenger, 'Die verschiedenen Systeme der Wassernutzung im

1. The Siloam channel
2. The Warren shaft
3. The Hezekiah tunnel

All three systems start from the Spring of Gihon, which rises on the eastern slope of the city halfway up above the Kidron Valley. Before the conquest of the city by David, access to the water supply was through the city gate, which was built above the spring along with the city wall in Middle Bronze Age II A.[19] There is no regular flow of water from the spring, but due to the particular geological conditions which prevail the water pours forth from a rock chamber at regular intervals. Thus in pre-Israelite times its exploitation probably necessitated the construction of a catchment basin.

Of the three systems, the Siloam channel runs more or less parallel with the city wall to a pond at the southern end of the city. The canal was partly sunk into the rock and covered with stone slabs, but partly also hewn out of the rock as a tunnel. Its purpose was to carry water to the gardens situated at the southern end of the city; thus it did not directly serve to supply the city with water.

On the basis of recent researches, the Warren shaft, named after its discoverer, is to be seen as the older of the two other systems. The date of its construction is unknown, but it may have been connected with the building measures carried out by Solomon; at any rate an earlier date, given its plan and the way in which it was constructed, is extremely improbable. The whole system was set out in such a way as to make use of natural holes in the rock, a fact which accounts for its irregularity. The access to the shaft is through the rock via a steep passage with a flight of steps, and a horizontal tunnel to the 13 m deep shaft; the spring water was channelled to the shaft by a tunnel 22 m in length. Thus on the one hand, it was impossible to ascend to the city from the spring, since the shaft presented an impassable obstacle. On the other hand, the use of the shaft was extremely arduous, since the water had to be brought up by leather buckets fastened to ropes. The possibility for drawing the water was thus limited; the excess water could be

südlichen Jerusalem und in Bezugnahme darauf in biblischen Texten', *UF* 14 (1983), pp. 279-94; but cf. the new investigation of Y. Shiloh, *Excavations at the City of David 1978–82* (Qedem 19; 1984), pp. 21-24.

19. It was uncovered by K.M Kenyon, *Jerusalem: Die heilige Stadt von David bis zu den Kreuzzügen* (1968), Pl. 11.

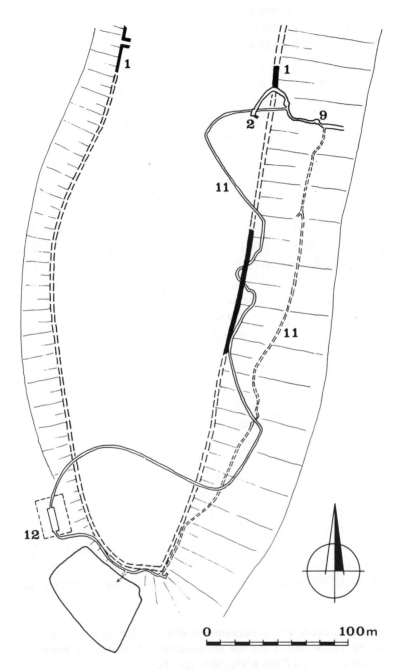

Figure 56. *Jerusalem. The water systems: 1. City wall. 2. Warren Shaft. 9. Gihon spring. 11. Hiskia tunnel. 11 (dotted line). Siloam channel. 12. Siloam pool.*

channelled via the Siloam channel into the gardens south of the city. This limited usefulness probably necessitated the planning and construction of a further system, which was named the Hezekiah tunnel after the king who built it.[20]

The Hezekiah tunnel was hewn through the rock; with a total length of 533 m, it has a gradient of 0.6 per cent. It ends in a newly-created basin, the so-called Pool of Siloam. Along its course, the tunnel makes several turns which are necessitated by several corrections to its direction. The collection basin was probably on the site of the present Pool of Siloam, and a further canal takes the overflow to the end of the Siloam channel, which was put out of function by the new tunnel. The tunnel has an average height of 2 m and a vaulted ceiling. The height of 5 m at the southern end is probably the result of a mistake made in the measurements that was corrected by further compensatory excavation of the bottom. This tunnel is undoubtedly the watercourse laid out by Hezekiah, which was given special mention in 2 Kgs 20.20. The new drawing point for the water was outside the existing wall, but Hezekiah refortified the south of the city with a new wall and brought the southeast hill inside the city precincts (cf. Chapter 6), so that the end of the tunnel came to be situated within the walls. The so-called Warren shaft water system remained in use and both systems were used down into Roman times, as is shown by additional building measures. The building inscription chiselled into the rock near the start of the Hezekiah tunnel praises the technical achievement of the undertaking, without however naming the builder.

The various systems for the provision of water constitute a considerable contribution towards the defences of the Israelite city. Their construction demanded a high level of technical know-how. This demonstrates a new element which has no predecessor in the Canaanite city. The Israelite city was thus given a further element of security, which in times of siege was of crucial importance when it was faced by the two alternatives of resistance or surrender. The construction of passages, shafts and tunnels was made possible by the use of iron tools,

20. For the layout cf. D. Ussishkin, 'The Original Length of the Siloam Tunnel in Jerusalem', *Levant* 8 (1976), pp. 82-95; N. Shaheen, 'The Siloam End of Hezekiah's Tunnel', *PEQ* 109 (1977), pp. 107-12; J. Wilkinson, 'The Pool of Siloam', *Levant* 10 (1978), pp. 33-51; N. Shaheen, 'The Sinuous Shape of Hezekiah's Tunnel', *PEQ* 111 (1979), pp. 103-108.

which were given a particular hardness through a special process. Thus the water supply systems are not only witness to a desire to survive, but also to progress in slowly developing technology.

Chapter 9

ECONOMY AND ADMINISTRATION

As in the prestate period the economy under the kings of Israel and
Judah was based on agriculture and animal husbandry. Farming activities were not limited to the planting of crops, but also included vineyards
and olive groves. Sheep and goats predominated amongst the animals
that were kept, even though cattle constituted about a quarter of all livestock reared. The predominance of any one type of animal was a consequence of local conditions in every case, with a mixed economy as the
basis. The production of foodstuffs broadly served to cover the requirements of each individual, but surpluses were naturally desirable and
could be exchanged for products which could not be home-produced
because the appropriate practical ability was lacking. In particular pottery, weapons and tools of bronze or iron, as well as jewellery, were
used as barter goods.

The Early Iron Age settlements permit recognition of a certain social
differentiation in that the private houses were of different sizes. However,
it seems that the differences of social class were not particularly marked
by the architecture, since the building that was carried out was, within a
certain range of variations, relatively homogeneous in nature. In spite of
this uniformity a society consisting of different levels can be assumed,
based on the variation in size of individual properties. Property means
land ownership, and the size of the land under cultivation determined
economic strength, on the basis of which social position was established.

The fact that large landowners already existed in prestate Israel can be
deduced from the narrative of Nabal in 1 Samuel 25. The marriage of
David to Abigail after the death of Nabal was certainly also intended to
bring the property of Nabal to him, and thus to enhance the economic
status which was a necessary prerequisite for his advancement. Only a
man who was economically independent and owned a sufficiently large
property could become king of the Israelite tribes, as is shown by the

example of Saul. Thus the ownership of land was a decisive factor in the matter of kingship before the establishment of the Davidic dynasty. By the same token the handing over of Ziklag by Achis of Gat to David to be held in fee (1 Sam. 27.6) constituted a decisive strengthening of his position, since the ownership of the whole village made David economically independent.[1]

The Administration

With the establishment of the kingship, a territorial state was created which encompassed the remaining Canaanite city states as well as the Israelite tribes. Through the formation of the state the tribes which were previously independent were drawn together to form a political unit. The rule of a central power embodied in the king stood in direct contradiction to the individual way of life enjoyed by the tribes. In the prestate period the village community was a self-sufficient and independent economic unit; its only obligation to the tribe was that of answering the summons to arms in the event of the 'Yahweh war'. The establishment of the kingship meant the creation of a completely new office, responsible for the organization of the tribes and the imposition of a state constitution over the tribal constitution. The kingship suspended the political autonomy of the tribes. It is only against this background that the new foundation of numerous cities can be explained. The new state required the settlement form of the city as a necessary defensive measure, and the open settlement was abandoned in favour of the fortified city. One measure carried out by the kingship led to the relocation of numerous villages, whereby the village community became the inhabitants of a city. The former self-sufficiency of the village community was now limited, since apart from the self-government carried on in all matters of civil law, the central administration dealt with all questions of taxation and defence through its crown civil servants. The extent and significance of these measures can be adduced from the lists of holders of the highest

1. The location of Ziklag has not yet been determined. *Khirbet el-Meshâh* can be excluded as a possibility, since the site was not occupied during the ninth and eighth centuries, as opposed to F. Crüsemann, 'Überlegungen zur Identifikation der *Hirbet el-Mšāš (Tel Māšōš)*', *ZDPV* 89 (1973), pp. 211-24. The identification with *Tell eš-Šerī'ā* is not certain, as this tell also exhibits a long gap in occupation during Iron Age II. The best candidate for Ziklag is *Tell es-Seba'*, although this however has been identified with Beersheba by Y. Aharoni.

offices which have been preserved from the reigns of David and Solomon in 2 Sam. 8.15-18 and 1 Kgs 4.1-6.[2] The holders of these offices cover all the important areas of government, cult, defence and the king's court. They were totally responsible for their areas of influence and were absolutely loyal to the reigning monarch. In the case of priests and scribes, the offices were hereditary. Altogether, the areas of influence of the various offices at the time of Solomon give a good insight into the administration of the kingdom. The offices of 'priest', 'scribe', 'speaker', 'commander of the army', 'in charge of the governors', 'friend of the king', 'in charge of the house' and 'in charge of forced labour' were given to their holders as titles; this is also shown by occasional finds of seal impressions.

The highest priest of the newly-built temple was actually the king, who was entitled to carry out sacrifices at any time. In practice, however, the king only exercised his priestly office on particular occasions, so that the priest in the lineage of the Zadokids was responsible for the regular offering of the sacrifice in the state shrine. 'Scribe' and 'speaker' were two offices instituted by David and based on Egyptian models. The scribe was not only in charge of the royal archive, that is of the writing of annals and deeds, but also for the conduct of correspondence inside the country as well as that with neighbouring states. He was probably also in charge of the scribes' school, the existence of which is not mentioned anywhere in the case of Jerusalem but can be presupposed on the grounds of ancient Near Eastern models.[3] The sphere of influence must have increased markedly with the expansion of the administration and international contacts, although written documents have not been preserved. The office of 'scribe' is not defined more clearly, but the scribe was perhaps the actual secretary of state who had to ensure that royal commands were carried out and legal judgments observed.

The position of commander of the army had already been created by Saul; the holder of the title under David was Joab, who was the most

2.   Cf. here I.N. Mettinger, *Solomonic State Officials* (1971); U. Rüterswörden, *Die Beamten der israelitischen Königszeit* (BWANT 117; 1985).

3.   A. Falkenstein, 'Die babylonische Schule', *Saeculum* 4 (1953), pp. 125-36; S.N. Kramer, *Die Sumerische Schule* (Wissenschaftliche Zeitschrift der Martin-Luther Universität Halle—Wittenberg; Gesellschafts- und sprachwissenschaftliche Reihe 5; 1955/6), pp. 695-704; H. Brunner, *Altägyptische Erziehung* (1957); H.-J. Hermisson, *Studien zur altisraelitischen Spruchweisheit* (WMANT 28; 1968), pp. 97-136.

powerful man in the state after the king himself. This can be adduced from the fact that he is mentioned first of all in the list dating from the time of David. Military conscription had probably already been replaced by the establishment of a professional army during the reign of Solomon. The commander of the army was the commander-in-chief in peacetime, while at times of war the king often took over the command of the army himself in battle, or when a siege was planned. The office of 'in charge of the governors' marks an innovation by Solomon, which can best be characterized as the introduction of taxation. Before that, David had continued to meet the requirements of the royal house from crown possessions. In order to satisfy the growing requirements of the court, the administration, and the army Solomon created twelve tax districts, of which each took on the responsibility of provisioning for one month (1 Kgs 4.7-19). The geographical definition of these twelve provinces took into account the former tribal areas, but excluded Judah for some unknown reason. In the coastal plain and in the plain of Jesreel the Canaanite cities were put together to form several provinces.[4]

The newly-created honorary title of 'friend of the king' had its parallel in the Egyptian title 'acquaintance of the king';[5] this was an official adviser in all areas of kingship. The holder of the title 'in charge of the house' was responsible for the royal possessions, which included large properties. Forced labour under its own overseer came into being because of the need to procure a work force for royal construction programmes. Although forced labour had already been introduced by David, Solomon was the first to develop this type of service on a large scale, in order to realize his ambitious building programmes.

Apart from these offices mentioned in the lists there are three others mentioned in the scriptures and known from seals. These are 'son of the king', 'the king's servant' and 'ruler of the city'.[6] Despite the occasional mention of holders of the offices their exact function is not clear. The designation 'son of the king' does not necessarily have to refer to a member of the royal family, but can also be a title conferred by the

4. For the division into provinces by Solomon cf. A. Alt, *Israels Gaue unter Salomo, Kleine Schriften II* (1953), pp. 76-89; G.E. Wright, 'The Provinces of Solomon', *Eretz Israel* 8 (1967), pp. 58*-68*; Y. Aharoni, 'The Solomonic Districts', *Tel Aviv* 3 (1976), pp. 5-15; H.N. Rösel, 'Zu den "Gauen" Salomos', *ZDPV* 100 (1984), pp. 84-90.

5. H. Donner, 'Der "Freund des Königs"', *ZAW* 73 (1961), pp. 269-77.

6. Cf. N. Avigad, *Hebrew Bullae from the Time of Jeremiah* (1986), Nr. 1-10.

king.[7] The office holders who are mentioned by name belong to the royal court and carry out measures which belong to the sphere of internal security; it seems that they were given a 'policing' brief. The actual duties of the 'servant of the king' are also not capable of closer definition; possibly this designation indicates a close connection with the king's own person. The title 'ruler of the city' is only met in connection with the capital cities of Jerusalem and Samaria (2 Kgs 23.8; 2 Chron. 34.8 and 1 Kgs 22.26). Since the kings were the actual rulers of the cities they had conquered or founded, this is probably an office created by them for the purpose of the administration of the capital.

The Social Order

The kingship thus brought basic changes for the people which at that time could only be understood as restrictions. Thus the various reports of the creation of the kingship of Saul in 1 Samuel 9–12 also indicate an attempt to justify the establishment of a king in various ways.[8] Amongst these reports, which vary in their intention and style, there is a text in the form of the so-called 'rights of the King' in 1 Sam. 8.11-17, which describes the effects of the kingship as an attack on the rights of the individual:

> 'This will be the sort of king who will govern you', he said. 'He will take your sons and make them serve in his chariots and with his cavalry, and will make them run before his chariot. Some he will appoint officers over units of a thousand and units of fifty. Others will plough his fields and reap his harvest; others again will make weapons of war and equipment for mounted troops. He will take your daughters for perfumers, cooks, and confectioners, and will seize the best of your cornfields, vineyards, and olive-yards, and give them to his lackeys. He will take a tenth of your grain and your vintage to give to his eunuchs and lackeys. Your slaves, both men and women, and the best of your cattle and your asses he will seize and put to his own use. He will take a tenth of your flocks, and you yourselves will become his slaves.'

7. Cf. G. Brin, 'The Title *bn (h)mlk* and its Parallels', *Annali dell'Instituto Orientale Universitario di Napoli* 29 (1969), pp. 433-56; A.F. Rainey, 'The Prince and the Pauper', *UF* 7 (1975), pp. 427-32; A. Lemaire, 'Note sur le titre *BN HMLK* dans l'ancien Israël', *Semitica* 29 (1979), pp. 59-65.
8. Cf. V. Fritz, 'Die Deutungen des Königtums Sauls in den Überlieferungen von seiner Entstehung 1 Samuel 9–11', *ZAW* 88 (1976), pp. 346-62.

This picture of the total supremacy of the king over the individual and the description of the situation of a population subject to royal caprice implies a criticism of the monarchy, which is drawn from the ideal of the prestate period without the rule of a king. The substance of this criticism is not only the restriction on freedom, but also the economic demand made on the people by the king, as manifested in the measures concerned with administration. The kingship brings the Israelite various obligations that were hitherto unknown and affect not only his independence but also his income. Detailed mention is made of military service, duties, collection of property and taxation. All these rights of the king mean an economic restriction for the Israelite, for he is now no longer master where his own productivity is concerned or sole beneficiary of the fruits of his labour.

As a new element, the kingship was not only bound to have had a decisive effect on the social structure, but there were also economic consequences connected with its establishment, consequences which arose from the position of the king on the one hand and from the existence of an administration connected with the central government on the other. The consequences of the kingship for the social structure have been examined by Albrecht Alt, who has recorded the 'occurrence of a non-uniform social and economic order'.[9] The restructuring of the social order was mainly brought about by the change in conditions of property ownership. In order to maintain his court and those dependent upon him the king had no other choice but to demand the necessary means from the rest of the people, and to secure the largest possible amount of property in the form of land for himself and his officials. As the kingship necessitated an attack on the property of the individual, it had, in the long term, to lead to a restructuring of the conditions of ownership and thus to the creation of a new social structure. This development is not the result of a definite policy, but it is an unavoidable process.

In order to meet economic obligations, the kings brought in changes which, although they did not alter the basis of the economy, transformed the conditions of property ownership and with them the social order. Among these changes was the introduction of crown property, the introduction of levies, and the obligation of service.

9. A. Alt, *Der Anteil des Königtums an der sozialen Entwicklung in den Reichen Israel und Juda, Kleine Schriften zur Geschichte des Volkes Israel*, III (1959), pp. 348-72.

Crown Property

Crown property comprises the land belonging to the crown, that is to say, the king's property. Even if the first kings did not acquire the throne by reason of an economic hegemony alone, there can be no doubt that Saul and David and all the remaining kings after them owned extensive lands. There is scant reference to royal lands, however, and only the control of David over the inheritance which came to him from Saul and the story of Naboth's vineyard in 1 Kings 21 give an incidental insight into legal questions connected with the royal ownership of land. The decisions made by David in connection with the property formerly belonging to Saul allows recognition of the fact that the king could give his property in feudal tenure; cf. 2 Samuel 9 and 16.1-14; 19.30. David provided for Meribaal, the son of Jonathan and the last remaining member of the line of Saul, a part of the property which had formerly belonged to Saul. Further references to this practice are absent, and it seems questionable whether feudalism was widespread in Israel. The story of Naboth's vineyard in 1 Kings 21 shows that the king could not increase his property at will.[10] The king only acquired the property of those who had been sentenced for crimes punishable by death. In the case of Naboth, Ahab did not balk at a legal murder in order to obtain the coveted vineyard, a fact which the Israelite social order and its concept of justice, as embodied by the prophets, could not accept.

The crown property was administered by royal officials and probably not given in feudal tenure. In the list in 1 Chron. 27.25-31 those in charge of the individual crown properties are listed specifically according to their area of responsibility. This list dates from the time of David and there is no reason to doubt its historical authenticity.[11] The type and

10. Cf. K. Baltzer, 'Naboths Weinberg (1 Kön 21)', *Wort und Dienst* 8 (1965), pp. 73-88; F.I. Andersen, 'The Socio-Juridicial Background of the Naboth Incident', *JBL* 85 (1966), pp. 46-57; O.H. Steck, *Überlieferung und Zeitgeschichte in den Elia-Erzählungen* (1968), pp. 32-77; P. Welten, 'Naboths Weinberg (1 Könige 21)', *EvT* 33 (1973), pp. 18-32; H. Seebass, 'Der Fall Naboth in I Reg. XXI', *VT* 24 (1974), pp. 474-88; E. Würthwein, 'Naboth-Novelle und Elia-Wort', *ZTK* 75 (1978), pp. 375-97.

11. The list in 1 Chron. 27.25-31 has not itself been examined to date and is seldom considered in connection with the picture presented by the reign of David. Although there are fundamental reasons for doubt in connection with the peculiar nature of the chronological evidence associated with it, there is at present no reason

nature of the crown property is clear from it. Apart from the details about the storage of provisions and the supervision of the workers, the following are mentioned as possessions of the king: arable land, vineyards, plantations with olive trees and fig trees, farms for cattle, camels, donkeys and small livestock. Apart from the production of wine and oil there is thus animal husbandry and the rearing of animals for transport. In the case of cattle, two different locations are expressly mentioned, but the rest of the property would also have been spread over the whole country. While the Israelite farmer, as a self-provider, was forced to carry on the different tasks of arable farming and livestock-rearing at the same time, the king could make intensive use of his land for monoculture on a large scale. The property of the king was not the only economic basis of the kingdom and was by no means sufficient for the provisioning of the court, but in every case it strengthened the economic hegemony of the king and had an importance that was by no means of little account as far as the royal income was concerned.

As a great landowner the king also enjoyed a position of economic power. Every king took over the property of his predecessor, while during the course of the monarchy the crown property steadily increased by the legal acquisition of ownerless property. Thus it was no longer the village council but the crown which administered land that acquired ownerless status. In addition the kings also took possession of new, hitherto unsettled land in the areas which had been won during the course of the formation of the state. Whether cities also counted among crown properties is unknown, but the possibility cannot be excluded.

Levies

The crown properties alone cannot have provided adequately for the growing needs of the court. Solomon divided up the provinces with the intention of providing the royal house with the necessary supplies (1 Kgs 4.7-19). Each of the twelve provinces was responsible for the provisioning of the royal house for one month of the year. The daily needs of the royal table are described in detail in 1 Kgs 5.2-3: '30 Kor of grain and 60 Kor of flour, 10 fat cattle and 20 cattle from the pasture as well as 100 head of livestock, apart from the fallow deer, gazelles, roe deer and fattened geese.'

to doubt its authenticity. Cf. P. Welten, *Geschichte und Geschichtsdarstellung in den Chronikbüchern* (WMANT 42; 1973), pp. 25-26.

There is no record of how these large quantities were acquired. Since all of the provinces with the exception of Judah were burdened equally with the responsibility of provisioning, the onus of providing the supplies can only have been shared amongst the entire population. The governors of the twelve provinces were thus at the same time the chief tax collectors, and were responsible for the levying, storage and delivery of the various agricultural products, cattle and game. There is no mention at all of oil and wine; they probably came from the crown properties. Thus the administrative measures of Solomon included the comprehensive taxation of the entire population for the upkeep of the court and all dependent upon it. Not only all the king's officials belonged to the court, but also the chariot divisions created by him, his bodyguard and his servants.

Since the taxes were remitted in kind, comprehensive storage facilities were necessary. Amongst the buildings the storage places near the garrisons are expressly mentioned (cf. 1 Kgs 9.19). Actual buildings for storage in Israel are only attested to in the vicinity of the palace at Lachish (cf. fig. 36). As throughout the whole of the ancient Near East, these were long, extensive rooms situated next to each other in large numbers.

The division of Judah into twelve provinces is also attested in the period after the division of the kingdom (Josh. 15.21-62 and 18.21-28).[12] Even if the purpose of this administrative measure is not given, it must have been connected with the creation of tax districts. The date of this division of Judah is the subject of controversy, but it probably took place before the Assyrian conquest in the eighth century during the ninth century.

There is no mention anywhere of the quantity of goods to be delivered. Only in the so-called king's rights in 1 Sam. 8.15 is there mention of the one tenth which probably thus constituted the level of the tax during the whole of the period of the monarchy.

In connection with taxation there are two important sources of inscription. These are the ostraka from Samaria and stamp impressions

12. Cf. A. Alt, 'Judas Gaue unter Josia', *Kleine Schriften zur Geschichte des Volkes Israel*, II (1953), pp. 276-88; F.M. Cross and G.E. Wright, 'The Boundary and Province Lists of the Kingdom of Judah', *JBL* 75 (1956), pp. 202-26; Z. Kallai-Kleinmann, 'The Town Lists of Juda, Simeon, Benjamin and Dan', *VT* 8 (1958), pp. 134-60 and *VT* 11 (1961), pp. 223-27: Y. Aharoni, 'The Province List of Judah', *VT* 9 (1959), pp. 225-46; Aharoni, *The Land of the Bible*, pp. 347-56.

on jar handles. The interpretation of both types of inscription is extremely difficult and several renderings have already been put forward. The ostraka from Samaria were discovered in a building next to the royal palace; these comprised short notes about deliveries of oil and wine with the year of the reign of an unnamed king, as well as the sender and receiver of the goods. The ostraka can be subdivided into two groups, namely those with the name of a village and those with the name of a tribe which sent the goods. Here, various distributors could deliver goods to the same recipient.[13] The latter were probably court officials. There is dispute, however, as to whether they received the goods from their own property for personal use or whether they passed on these levies to the court. The texts do not give any information on this matter. With a view to parallel practices in Ugarit, A.F. Rainey is of the opinion that the ostraka from Samaria constitute 'receipts' for deliveries from the property of high officials, whereby this property could also be land which the king had given to his officials to be held in tenure.[14] The location of the find belies this opinion, since the receipt of deliveries made to the royal court was most probably connected with its provisioning. Thus the ostraka can probably be understood as 'accompanying documents' for the dues delivered by individual families and tribes to the royal house; these would later be recorded in lists.[15]

The stamp impressions on jar handles, of which several hundred have

13. A translation and survey is offered by Aharoni, *The Land of the Bible*, pp. 356-68.

14. A.F. Rainey, 'Administration in Ugarit and the Samaria Ostraca', *IEJ* 12 (1962), pp. 62-63; 'The Land Grant System at Ugarit and its Wider Near Eastern Setting', *Fourth World Congress of Jewish Studies*, I (1967), pp. 187-91; *idem*, 'The Samaria Ostraca in the Light of Fresh Evidence', *PEQ* 99 (1967), pp. 32-41; *idem*, 'Semantic Parallels to the Samaria Ostraca', *PEQ* 102 (1970), pp. 45-51; 'The *Sitz im Leben* of the Samaria Ostraca', *Tel Aviv* 6 (1979), pp. 91-94. The supposition by Y. Yadin, that those persons listed with accompanying prepositions were not the recipients but the owners, cannot stand. Cf. Y. Yadin, 'Recipients or Owners: A Note on the Samaria Ostraca', *IEJ* 9 (1959), pp. 184-87; *idem*, 'A Further Note on the Samaria Ostraca', *IEJ* 12 (1962), pp. 64-66, cf. the refutation by A.F. Rainey, 'Private Seal Impressions: a Note on Semantics', *IEJ* 16 (1966), pp. 187-90.

15. Cf. W.H. Shea, 'The Date and Significance of the Samaria Ostraca', *IEJ* 27 (1977), pp. 16-27; F.M. Cross, 'Ammonite Ostraca from Heshbon', *Andrew University Seminary Studies* 13 (1975), pp. 8-10. The difficult question of the dating does not need to be discussed here, cf. A.F. Rainey, 'Toward a Precise Date for the Samaria Ostraca', *BASOR* 272 (1988), pp. 69-74.

been found in various places in Judah, prove to be extremely friable material, and can only be categorized with uncertainty.[16] The stamps were impressed on the handles of storage jars before firing and bear the notation *lmlk* 'belonging to the king', and the name of one of four places—Hebron, Sif, Socho or *mmšt*. Apart from the inscription there is the symbol of a winged scarab, whereby differentiation can be made between two-winged and four-winged scarabs. As D. Ussishkin has now demonstrated, some jars bear private seals on one or two other handles, in addition to these official seals.[17] This not only limits their ownership to one city, but to one individual person. The stamping of the vessels before firing represents an official marking; thus they belonged not to a private person but were royal property and served to provision official places in various locations. It is not clear here who was supplied with provisions and whence the provisions themselves originated. It can most probably be assumed that the deliveries went to officials appointed by the crown or to troops in various parts of the country. Where the origin of the provisions is concerned either crown property or tax receipts may be considered. As apart from *mmšt* the existence of the cities named as Hebron, Sif, and Socho is well attested, it can most likely be assumed that they served as administrative centres for the royal authority. In that case, the goods transported could hardly have originated from crown property, which could have been directly delivered, but from goods collected as dues which were stored there and sent out as required. The four cities were thus the seat of the authority responsible for the levy of taxes for a certain area.[18] The persons named on the private seals could perhaps have been royal tax officials.

Forced Labour

In addition to the obligation of levies on agricultural products and animal rearing the Israelite also had an obligation of service to the king. In the historical notes in the Books of the Kings two expressions are used for villeinage or forced labour, of which one is used to describe the forced

16. P. Welten, *Die Königs-Stempel* (1969); H.D. Lance, 'The Royal Stamps and the Kingdom of Josiah', *HTR* 64 (1971), pp. 316-32.
17. D. Ussishkin, 'Royal Judean Storage Jars and Private Seal Impressions', *BASOR* 223 (1976), pp. 1-13.
18. Thus Aharoni, *The Land of the Bible*, pp. 394-400.

labour carried out by the non-Israelite element of the population.[19] Of the inhabitants of the Canaanite cities already incorporated into the greater kingdom of David, 10,000 men from each city had to work for one month in the Lebanon and each was then allowed to carry on his own work for two months at home (1. Kgs 5.27-28). In a similar way to the Canaanite element of the population, the Israelites were also obliged to render their services. 70,000 carriers and 80,000 stone masons are named as workers who were watched over by officials (1 Kgs 5.29-30), but these figures seem to have been greatly exaggerated.

An attempt was made as early as 1 Kgs 9.22 to release the Israelites from forced labour; here it is stated that 'Solomon did not permit the enslavement of any of the Israelites. They were soldiers and his servants and his commanders and those set to fight with his war chariots, and the commanders of his war chariots and horses.' This note constitutes a social classification corresponding to the elements in the population. How little this division corresponded to the real state of affairs is demonstrated by the confrontations over the burden of taxation and services to be rendered after the death of Solomon. While forced labour is not specifically mentioned in the negotiations between the northern tribes and Rehoboam in 1 Kings 12, but only 'labour' in general is mentioned, the dispatch of Adoniram, the official in charge of forced labour, shows that the question of obligatory service must have played a decisive role in the controversy over the recognition of Rehoboam as successor to Solomon. Even if the division of Solomon's kingdom had to do with the former differences between north and south,[20] economic factors also contributed to this split. Jeroboam, the first king of the northern kingdom, was himself once one of Solomon's officials in charge of the forced labour in the house of Joseph (1 Kgs 11.28) and would have made concessions to the northern tribes in matters of taxation and services to be rendered which Rehoboam had denied the people.

Thus the king had the right to certain work quotas from the people. Solomon used this labour potential for his building programmes. But not only the royal monumental buildings such as temples and palaces in Jerusalem or the palace of the royal representative in Megiddo were constructed by this method; the numerous building projects designed for the defence of the country were also thus carried out. Not only the cities

19. A.F. Rainey, 'Compulsory Labour Gangs in Ancient Israel', *IEJ* 20 (1970), pp. 191-202.

20. Cf. B. Halpern, 'Sectionalism and the Schism', *JBL* 93 (1974), pp. 519-32.

supplying horses and chariots and the cities supplying provisions in general are mentioned in allusions to Solomon's building activities, but also the construction work at Gezer, lower Beth-Horon, Baalat and Tamara are given specific mention (1 Kgs 9.17-19).[21] Of this building activity, only the six-chamber gate at Gezer including a section of the casemate wall has been excavated to date.[22] No excavation has yet taken place at the other towns mentioned, and the rest of the cities named as having a particular function cannot as yet be identified. The reference shows, however, that the cities had to assume particular functions where administration or military matters were concerned.

A further note firmly establishes that building works were carried on in Jerusalem and that Hazor, Megiddo and Gezer were fortified (1 Kgs 9.15). In addition to the city gate at Gezer the remains of Solomon's building activities in Hazor Stratum X B and Megiddo Stratum V A have been uncovered (cf. figs 27, 30). Both cities differ considerably from one another. While a large six-chamber gate and a strong casemate wall were built at Hazor, the fortification at Megiddo is limited to a ring of houses and a small two-chamber gate, though palace 1723 is a manifestation of royal power.

Apart from the locations named above, Solomon also fortified numerous cities. Thus in the final analysis compulsory service contributed to the security of the country and the well-being of the people. At the beginning of the period of the monarchy, the fortified city replaced the mostly unfortified and thus defenceless settlements of the prestate period. A whole system of city foundations secured the country from attack by hostile neighbours. In the post-Solomon period the construction of fortifications would have continued to be a task carried out by

21. Lower Beth-Horon (*Bēt 'Ūr et-tahta*) was situated in the mountains, on the important stretch of land rising up from the coastal plain. The location of Baalat cannot be positively identified, but was certainly in the area to the south or west of Gezer, after Josh. 19.44. Tamar is to be placed in *'Ēn Hasb* on the western edge of the northern Arabah, cf. Y. Aharoni, 'Tamar and the Roads to Elath', *IEJ* 13 (1963), pp. 30-42.

22. Cf. Y. Yadin, 'Solomon's City Wall and Gate at Gezer', *IEJ* 8 (1958), pp. 80-86. The later excavations have not yet provided a definite date for the so-called outer wall, cf. W.G. Dever, 'Late Bronze Age and Solomonic Defenses at Gezer: New Evidence' , *BASOR* 262 (1986), pp. 9-34, with I. Finkelstein, 'The Date of Gezer's Outer Wall', *Tel Aviv* 8 (1981), pp. 136-45; A. Zertal, 'The Gates of Gezer', *Eretz Israel* 15 (1981), pp. 222-28 (in Hebrew); S. Bunimovitz, 'Glacis 10 014 and Gezer's Late Bronze Age Fortifications', *Tel Aviv* 10 (1983), pp. 61-70.

the whole community. The compulsory service described as forced labour was thus introduced to carry out the measures necessary for defence, quite apart from royal building programmes.

Consequences

Before the formation of the states the Israelite farmers produced enough to meet their own needs. Tools and pottery were paid for by goods in kind, and all other consumer articles were produced within the family. The village community was thus an economically self-sufficient and independent unit. The cultivation of the land ensured the existence of each individual, and the income corresponded to the varying size of each property.

The tribes achieved political independence with the monarchy, but this new form of state meant a considerable change in economic conditions. The king not only had political but also economic power. His own property, taxes and services ensured him a position of supremacy, which of course was indispensable for the carrying out of the tasks connected with the monarchy. Among these was not only the provisioning of all the members of the royal court, but also the upkeep of the troops and the carrying out of building measures.

The establishment of the monarchy meant an economic burden for the Israelite farmer, since now a part of the agricultural production had to be given to the crown. The necessary dues could only be compensated for by increased cultivation or savings where private consumption was concerned. Thus the tax measures must above all have affected the small farmer, who could neither increase the size of his property at will, nor raise his agricultural productivity. The obligation to render taxes thus led in individual cases to the necessity of incurring debts and also to enslavement. The economic upper class by contrast could compensate for the burden of taxation by increased cultivation and therefore increased its economic potential. The farmers who became dependent because of debts incurred were thus available as a slave workforce to this class of large landowners.

On the whole, an economic upturn can be demonstrated in the early period of the monarchy. This is attested mainly by the new settlement that took place in many locations which had either remained uninhabited or been only temporarily inhabited since their destruction at the end of the Late Bronze Age. Numerous cities were provided with a ring of walls and a new population in the period of David and Solomon. Thus a territorial expansion was connected with the formation of the states, and this was manifested in the newly-founded cities.

Chapter 10

EVERYDAY LIFE

With the exception of the capital cities, in which the king enjoyed far-reaching rights, and with the exception of the fortresses, which were directly under royal control, the Israelite cities were self-governing in all legal and economic matters. This self-government is a legacy of the tribal constitutions of the prestate period, according to which both the tribe as well as the smaller units of clan and family had a right to independent decision-making in all matters which affected them. After the formation of the state this social structure—a tribal-orientated organization on the basis of equality of all members under the law—was retained. The population in the newly-founded cities thus corresponds to the former village community where independence is concerned, except that obligations to the king had to be fulfilled as an additional service. Other conditions may perhaps be presupposed to have existed in the case of the former Canaanite cities which had been incorporated into the kingdom, but more exact details are unknown because of a lack of written sources; for the same reason the social structure itself cannot be more closely described. How stubbornly a free Israelite was able to defend his tribal rights is shown in the account in 1 Kings 21.

There is no indication from the texts of a structured population in the city.[1] It is clear, however, that the elders of the city who are given occasional mention (1 Sam. 16.4; 30.26ff.) were holders of an office and members of a committee concerned with the execution of clearly defined tasks within the framework of the community. The elders were probably the heads of the clans or families resident in the cities. Their authority was primarily concerned with the maintenance of internal order, the representation of the city elsewhere and the conduct of local

---

1. Cf. J. Pedersen, *Israel. Its Life and Culture*, I-IV (1926/40); L. Köhler, *Der hebräische Mensch* (repr., 1976 [1953]).

justice.[2] According to the sources the meeting of the elders took place at
the gate, which thus acquired a civil function (cf. Ruth 4.1-11). Public
buildings, which could have served for a council meeting, are not as yet
extant from the period of the monarchy; thus one of the chambers in the
gate probably served as a location for the meetings of the elders. This is
supported by the archaeological find of benches which ran around the
walls of the gate chambers as in the gates at *Tell es-Seba'* Stratum II
and in Kinneret Stratum II.[3] Thus in the cities the elders represented the
population. Only in the capital cities of Jerusalem and Samaria, under the
influence of a social structure which had changed because of the monarchy, did they become a part of the upper class together with the other
holders of public office.[4]

The inhabitants of the cities were mostly farmers; it was only in the
cities which had a limited administrative or military function that
members of the standing army were accommodated in buildings especially constructed for the purpose. We know nothing about the length of
their service, the form of payment they received and their later reinte-
gration into society.[5] The main purpose of the stationing of troops is to
maintain the security of an area and the borders; in particular they were
used on military expeditions, while the defence of the city in case of
attack by an enemy was primarily the obligation of the inhabitants.

As farmers, the inhabitants cultivated fields and gardens in the vicinity
of the city. In order to carry out their agricultural activities, the men left
the city in the morning, and returned in the evening within the protection of the walls. This daily rhythm was probably interrupted on the
seventh day of the week, the Sabbath, which had already been designated a day of rest at an early date. This pattern of a continuous week of
seven days and the interruption of work on the last day of the week is

2.   Because of the variations in development the conditions in other cities in the
East can only be used for comparison with extreme care. However, there seems to
have been a parallel in the border areas of the Kingdom of Ulari, cf. H. Klengel, 'Zu
den *šībutum* in altbabylonischer Zeit', *Orientalia* ns 29 (1960), pp. 357-75.
3.   Cf. Y. Aharoni, *Tel Aviv* 1 (1974), pp. 37-39; V. Fritz, *Tel Aviv* 20 (1993),
p. 199.
4.   The wider significance of the Elders and the opinions connected with it as
expressed in Hebrew literature need not be brought into discussion here; cf.
B. Halpern, *The Emergence of Israel in Canaan* (1983), pp. 199-205; H. Reviv, *The
Elders in Ancient Israel* (1983).
5.   On the composition of the army cf. F. Nötscher, *Biblische Altertumskunde*
(1940), pp. 145-56; the question of armament need not be examined here.

quite unique in the ancient Near East and has to be seen as a genuinely Israelite phenomenon.[6] The origin and the original purpose of this unique division of the week is unknown.

As in every agricultural society the work to be done at any time was determined by the season of the year. Plowing and sowing, planting and harvesting, threshing and treading of grapes were all connected with a certain time of the year. In the so-called farmer's calendar from Gezer, the year was divided into twelve months according to the various agricultural tasks that were necessary, beginning in autumn:

> Two months are for bringing in produce;
> Two months are for sowing;
> Two months are for late sowing;
> One month is for cutting flax;
> One month is for cutting corn;
> One month is for cutting and measuring;
> Two months are for the wine harvest;
> One month is for the harvest of the fruits of summer.[7]

In a land characterized by mountains, the fields for cultivation were situated in the valleys and plains, while the vineyards and olive groves were positioned on the slopes, terraced for this purpose. The higher ranges of the mountains were forested and uninhabited. The large part of the mountain mass consists of different types of limestone, which erode to form the typical and highly fertile red-brown earth. Leaving aside the differing climatic conditions in the Negev and the Jordan valley, a Mediterranean climate predominates over the greater part of the country, characterized by dry summers and mild winters with adequate precipitation. In the areas which have a Mediterranean climate the cultivated fields received their water from rainfall; the steppes on the fringes of the cultivated land were only sporadically settled, since cultivation by irrigation channels was unknown until Roman times. The areas were, however, used for grazing.

The fertility of the country is reflected in the biblical description of 'the land flowing with milk and honey' (Exod. 3.8, 17; 13.5; 33.3 etc). The two products mentioned in this formula-like description indicate the

6. Cf. the examination and compilation of profuse evidence by J. Hehn, *Siebenzahl und Sabbat bei den Babyloniern und im Alten Testament* (1907).

7. H. Donner and W. Röllig, '*Kanaanäische und aramäische Inschriften*, I–III (1962–64), Nr. 182; cf. here S. Talmon, 'The Gezer Calendar and the Seasonal Cycle of Ancient Canaan', *JAOS* 83 (1963), pp. 177-87.

natural wealth of the country, and the picture it conjures up expresses the surplus of such resources. Even in the tale of Sinuhe the Egyptian, who sought refuge in Canaan at the beginning of the second millennium, a part of the country which cannot be identified is referred to as 'beautiful' and described with affection: 'There were figs and grapes; it possessed more wine than water, much honey and was rich in oil. Fruits of all kinds hung from its trees, there was barley, and wheat, and there were innumerable animals of all kinds'.[8] The reality of work on the land was surely otherwise. In ancient Israel, the labours of farming were already embodied in the order of creation. In the story of the banishment from the Garden of Eden in Gen. 3.17 the farmland 'shall bear you thorns and thistles'. Thorns and thistles indicate the heavy nature of the work, farming is bound up with effort and burden, and yield can only be achieved with sweat. Leaving aside the fertility of the land, the daily work of the farmer has realistically to be described as heavy.

By far the most important type of grain was barley, but wheat was also cultivated. Accordingly, barley bread was the main foodstuff (cf. Judg. 7.13; 2 Kgs 4.42). Lentils and peas are attested among those pulses which can be stored well.[9] The grain was sown in winter, from December to February, to allow it to grow throughout the spring when the ground was still damp from rainfall. Before sowing, the ground was tilled with a simple hook-plough, in order to break up the earth.[10] Finds of iron ploughshares prove that this important tool was kept in the houses (fig. 57). Cattle or donkeys served as draught animals, yoked singly or in pairs in front of the plough. To yoke a bull and a donkey together was expressly forbidden in Deut. 22.10. All other work in the fields was carried out with the hoe or mattock, which consisted of a piece of metal attached at a right angle to the handle, just as is still used in the Levant today.[11]

8.   E. Edel, in, Galling, *Textbuch zur Geschichte Israels*, p. 4; cf. here A.F. Rainey, 'The World of Sinuhe', *Israel Oriental Studies* 2 (1972), pp. 369-408.

9.   N. Liphschitz and Y. Waisel, in Y. Aharoni (ed.), *Beersheba*, I (1973), pp. 97-105, also 'Dendroarchaeological Investigations in Israel (Taanach)', *IEJ* 30 (1980), pp. 132-36.

10.   As the ploughs were made of wood they have not been preserved; however the Egyptian representations give a good illustration of what they were like, cf. W. Wreszinski, *Atlas zur altägyptischen Kulturgeschichte*, I (1923), Nr. 9.51.176.

11.   Until the inroads made by industrialization into agriculture the tools and implements had hardly changed in Palestine; thus the description given by G. Dalman for the period prior to the First World War offers a good picture, cf. G. Dalman,

Figure 57. Iron plough share from Kinneret (8th c. BC).

While the joys of the harvest were proverbial (cf. Isa. 9.2) the cutting of the corn was no less laborious than the tilling of the fields. The instrument of harvesting was the sickle, which was made of iron because of its superior sharpness (fig. 58). The size and shape of the sickle could vary considerably. As a rule, the ears were cut off quite high, so that the straw remained in the form of long stubble. The ears were bound into sheaves (cf. Gen. 37.7; Deut. 24.19; Judg. 15.5) and brought to the threshing floors on the backs of animals. The threshing floor was an open plateau on a rock or a trodden-down area, and was situated outside the city. To thresh the corn, either draught animals were driven over the grain, or the so-called threshing sledge was pulled over it (cf. Isa. 41.15; Hos. 10.11; Amos 1.3). Thereafter the material that had been threshed was winnowed, that is, thrown up into the wind, so that the grains separated from the lighter chaff. The grain extracted was then weighed, packed into sacks (cf. Gen. 42.25) and stored in boxes, pits or granaries.

Amongst the fruit-bearing trees, the olive takes first place (cf. Judg. 9.8-10). Apart from this, only the fig tree is given frequent mention but there were also pomegranates, apples, almond trees and date palms. The olive tree was primarily planted on the slopes of the mountains, which were protected from erosion by means of terrace walls.[12] The olive was—and still is today—harvested in late autumn and pressed to extract oil, after an intermediate period of storage. The

---

Arbeit und Sitte in Palästina, II (1932), pp. 242-304.

12. Terraces of cultivated trees characterize the landscape of the Transjordan even today. For their layout in the Iron Age cf. Z. Ron, 'Agricultural Terraces in the Judean Mountains', *IEJ* 16 (1966), pp. 33-49; 111-22; C.H.J. De Geus, 'The Importance of Archaeological Research into the Palestinian Agricultural Terraces', *PEQ* 107 (1975), pp. 65-74; G. Edelstein and M. Kislev, 'Mevasseret Yerushalayim. The Ancient Settlement and its Agricultural Terraces', *BA* 44 (1981), pp. 53-56.

Figure 58. *Iron sickle from* Khirbet el-Meshâsh *(11th c. BC).*

pressing was carried out in bowl-like hollows in the rocks in open areas or in specially hollowed-out round stones of considerable size, as have been found on *Tell Beit Mirsim*.[13] The oil was stored in large jars and was put to many uses in the preparation of food and the maintenance of personal hygiene.

The importance of wine in the life of the Israelites, as is reflected in the literature, is parallelled by the role of viticulture in the agrarian economy.[14] The expenditure involved in the setting up of a vineyard is expressly mentioned in Isa. 5.1-7. It is enclosed by a wall for protection and provided with a tower and a winepress. The vines were pruned back in the winter, the harvest began as early as August and was considered the happiest time of the year. The harvested grapes were pressed on the

13. The stones were falsely interpreted by the excavator as installations for the dye-works, cf. W.F. Albright, *The Excavations of Tell Beit Mirsim III. The Iron Age* (AASOR 21-22; 1943), pp. 60-62 with Plates 51-53. In contrast G. Dalman, *Arbeit und Sitte in Palästina*, V (1937), pp. 77-78 has already offered the correct interpretation as an olive-press.

14. Cf. J. Limbacher, *Weinbau in der Bibel* (1931); C. Seltman, *Wine in the Ancient World* (1957); G. Hagenow, *Aus dem Weingarten der Antike* (1982).

spot. The winepress, hewn out of the rock and situated either within the vineyard or nearby, consisted of a treading floor at a higher level and a collecting basin, the vat, at a lower level, into which the juice obtained from treading the grapes could flow. For further processing, the must or new wine was poured off into jars, in which the finished wine was also stored. For purposes of transport, the wine could be poured into animal skins (cf. Josh. 9.4, 13; 1 Sam. 1.24; 10.3; 25.18). According to the biblical view, wine made the heart of man rejoice, but its production was labour intensive, like all agricultural activities.

Among the animals kept, the draught animals and those used for riding, that is to say the donkey and the camel, are to be distinguished from the domestic animals, the cattle, sheep and goats.[15] Due to a lack of documentary evidence nothing can be said about the size of the herds but the ownership of a donkey or a camel would have been the exception and the number of domestic animals small. Cattle, sheep and goats were kept in enclosures outside the city. To what extent a shepherd watched over animals belonging to several owners is unknown. At any rate, the pastures were outside the area of the enclosures; it was only in the period between the harvest and the new sowing of the crop that the herds could be let into the fields. Stalls to accommodate the herds have not yet been found. Apart from providing milk, the animals were a source of meat. Slaughtering took place outside the city. Doves were kept for poultry, and played a great part in the imagery of the Bible (cf. Isa. 38.14; Pss. 55.7; Hos. 11.11; Nah. 2.8). An additional source of nourishment was available in the form of hunted game, such as deer or gazelle.

Farming was a full-time, all-year-round occupation, in which the inhabitants of the ancient Israelite city spent a large part of the day out of the house in the fields, the olive grove, the vineyard or with the herds. The Israelite was a self-provider, who tilled the land in order to feed himself and his family. How far he was able to produce a surplus is unknown; yields definitely fluctuated from year to year. Although the farmer produced everything himself, he must have exchanged some of his produce for other goods that he could not produce himself, quite apart from having to deliver his dues to the royal court. Among such goods were pottery, tools and jewellery made from iron and bronze, which could only be obtained through barter.

15. Cf. as an example the examination of the animal bones from Kinneret by R. Ziegler and J. Boessneck, 'Tierreste der Eisenzeit II', in V. Fritz, *Kinneret* (1990), pp. 133-58.

Since no craftsmen's workshops have been discovered in the cities to date, it has to be assumed that the workshops of both the potters and the smiths must have been situated outside the city.[16] Both of these crafts rely on large quantities of combustible material, thus the production sites may have been situated near an area of forest. The necessary vessels and tools were exchanged for the products of the land, just as was jewellery. Only at the royal court and among large landowners who possessed the appropriate wealth was it normal for money to change hands; when there was a shortage of minted coins, chopped-up silver pieces were weighed and used (cf. Gen. 23.16; Isa. 4.6; Jer. 32.10). The basic unit of currency was the shekel, which on the evidence of weights found measured 11.8 grammes; the corresponding value in products of the soil is unknown.[17] But the silver shekel must have had a high value, since the redemption price of a man was 50 shekels and that of a woman 30 shekels (Lev. 27.1-8). Long-distance trade was apparently a royal monopoly, a fact indirectly corroborated by the small number of imported finds.

By reason of the absence of the men, life in the city during the day was largely governed by the women. Even if the women took part in work on the land at times of necessity, for example during the harvest, their real station was to remain in the home and carry out domestic tasks. Apart from bringing up the children the activities of the women consisted mainly of preparing and providing food and clothing. Both of these are connected with the yield from the land, and humble circumstances meant that requirements were modest. The scholar Jesus Sirach, who lived in the second century BC mentioned the following as the only necessities of life: 'Water and fire and iron and salt, fat ears of wheat, milk, honey, the juice of the grape, oil and clothing' (39.26).

The diet was broadly vegetarian: bread, dairy products, honey, fruit and vegetables were the normal daily diet. 'To have a meal is to eat bread' (Gen. 37.25; 1 Sam. 20.24).[18] Meat was only eaten at feasts of

16. A summary and review of handcrafts is lacking. For ceramics cf. R. Amiran, *Ancient Pottery of the Holy Land* (1969).

17. Cf. on the unit value and marking of the shekel Y. Aharoni, 'The Use of Hieratic Numerals in Hebrew Ostraca and the Shekel Weights', *BASOR* (1984), 1966), pp. 13-19; Y. Yadin, 'Ancient Judean Weights and the Date of the Samaria Ostraca', *Scripta Hierosolymitana* 8 (1961), pp. 9-25.

18. On nutrition in antiquity cf. P. and D. Brothwell, *Manna und Hirse. Eine Kulturgeschichte der Ernährung* (1984).

sacrifice or on other festive occasions such as the birth of a son or a wedding. The main stage of preparation of the meal was the baking of bread; the corn had to be ground using a handmill and the dough mixed up in a basin. The flat rubbing stone of basalt, on which the grains were ground using another stone, belonged among the equipment possessed by every house. Barley bread was baked in the form of round flat cakes in an oven, of which there was one in every house. This dome-shaped mud oven was often not situated in the courtyard, but in the back room of the house. It had an opening on top through which it was fuelled with wood, and through which the smoke could also escape (fig. 59). As soon as the necessary temperature had been attained inside the oven, the flat cakes of dough were pressed against its inner walls and adhered to them during baking. Honey cakes (Exod. 16.31) and raisin cakes (1 Sam. 25.18; 2 Sam. 6.19) were baked as a special delicacy.

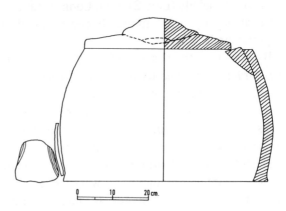

Figure 59. *Oven with cover in* Khirbet el-Meshâsh *(11th c. bc).*

The great majority of the clay cooking pots of different sizes found in the houses indicate that some of the meals were cooked. This is understandable in the case of pulses, as they are otherwise inedible, but it also applied to other kinds of vegetables. Meat was also cooked in pots (Exod. 27.3; 1 Sam. 2.13-14). Salt was used as a seasoning, since this was easily obtained from the Dead Sea, and the use of caraway, dill and coriander was known (Exod. 16.31; Num. 11.7; Isa. 28.25).

Milk and honey also counted among the daily foodstuffs, and were especially valued as delicacies. Honey, the only substance available for sweetening, originated from colonies of wild bees (1 Sam. 14.25ff.); it is not known to what degree bee-keeping was practised. Fresh milk or coagulated sour milk was a particularly refreshing drink; the rules of hospitality demanded that this should be offered to a guest. Cheese was also made from the milk (1 Sam. 17.18; 2 Sam. 17.29), but the type and manufacturing process is not described in greater detail. Whether butter was produced by filling animal skins with milk and shaking or beating them in the appropriate way is beyond our knowledge, since it cannot be definitely ascertained on the basis of Prov. 30.33.

Apart from providing for the nourishment of the family the making of clothes, blankets and sacks was the task of the women. The raw materials used were wool and flax. The wool had to be spun into yarn and the numerous spindle whorls and pieces of pottery with holes bored through them attest to the widespread custom of hand spinning.[19] After cutting, drying and combing the flax was also spun, and the threads further processed to make linen. Cloth was woven from both yarns, but whether they were used for knitting remains an open question at present.[20] The wool could be dyed using natural substances, and patterns woven into the material used for clothing.

Because of a lack of pictorial representations, the form of clothing predominant is unknown. However, despite a certain formalization the Assyrian and Egyptian monuments offer an exact representation of the reality of the time.[21] On the relief of Sennacherib in Niniveh two types of clothing can be differentiated among the representations of Judaeans: the shirt-like shift which reached down to the ankles and had short sleeves, and the wrap-over robe, which was made of a length of cloth, wrapped around the body and held together by a belt (fig. 60). The mode of dress was the same for both sexes, but there could be some differences. Women wore a headscarf in addition to the shirt-like shift, which reached down to the hem of the shift, and in the case of men the wrap-over robe could be limited to an apron, with the upper part of the body either covered by a short shirt-shift or completely naked. A narrow strip of cloth was used to cover the head, and this was bound

19. As an example cf. the pieces from Kinneret as mentioned in Fritz, *Kinneret*, Pl. 105 and 106.

20. The best possibilities for comparison are offered by the occupations still carried on in the country today, cf. G. Dalman, *Arbeit und Sitte in Palästina*, V (1937), pp. 94-144.

21. Cf. M. Wäfler, *Nicht-Assyrer neuassyrischer Darstellungen* (AOAT 26; 1975).

around the forehead over the hair, its free end hanging down over the shoulder from above the ear.

In the city, the home was at the centre of daily life, with the courtyard at its heart. The streets were narrow and winding and also served as a place for children to play, as long as they were not required to help with the necessary work. Shops and public places were unknown, so that people only had the opportunity to meet through occasional visits to each other or on the way to the well.

Figure 60. *Women and men from Lachish on the relief of Sennacherib in Ninive.*

Thus urban life was limited to the precincts of the house and governed by the necessity of providing food and clothing. An interruption in the daily rhythm was only provided by the various feasts. The Sabbath had a certain festive character, even if it only consisted of a rest from work and was celebrated without any further cultic celebration (Exod. 20.8-11). By contrast the day of the new moon was celebrated, and for this special provision for sacrifices was made within the festival calendar in Num. 28.11-15. Apart from the feast of New Year, the course of the year was determined by the three great feasts of Passover-Mazzot, the Feast of Weeks and the Feast of the Tabernacle, which were celebrated at the country sanctuaries; however by the end of the period of the monarchy they were celebrated exclusively at the Temple in Jerusalem (cf. Exod. 23.10-19; 34.18-26; Deut. 16.1-17).[22]

The year began in autumn, whereby the regular introduction of a thirteenth month provided a balance between the lunar calendar and the solar year. All feasts are determined by the annual rhythmn of nature, have a strong connection with agriculture and last for eight days. The Passover-Mazzot festival marks the beginning of spring and the corn harvest, the Feast of Weeks 50 days later coincides with the end of the corn harvest, and the Feast of the Tabernacle in autumn takes place at the time of the wine harvest. Traditionally they are connected with the decisive events in the early history of Israel—the Exodus, the revelations on Sinai and the wanderings in the desert—and have thus acquired a salvatory connotation which binds the individual with the history of his people and the powerful efficiency of his God manifested therein. The celebrations began with sacrifices and the eating of meat and were characteristically loud and happy occasions. Apart from religious feasts the wedding was an occasion of the greatest joy (cf. Jer. 7.34; 16.9; 25.10), which because of the large number of guests was not celebrated at home but in the immediate vicinity of the city.

With the exception of the feasts, life was carried on under what were rather impoverished circumstances; a modest luxury was to be found in the palaces of the king and his official representatives. Apart from the small upper class, which was given security through the possession of

22. A summary is given in H.-J. Kraus, *Gottesdienst in Israel* (2nd edn, 1962). The post-exile festivals of Purim and Hanukka must be left out of discussion here. The Day of Atonement, characterized by fasting, can also be left out because of its penitential character.

large areas of land, the population of the cities appears as a relatively homogeneous agrarian society. The urban inhabitants are for the most part farmers, and soldiers or officials were only found in the cities with administrative or military functions. Thus as a rule, the city-dweller was involved in agriculture in order to feed his own family. As handicrafts and trade were only carried on to a modest extent, there was no differentiated social order within the city in ancient Israel, apart from the society in the capital cities and administrative centres. This far-reaching equality is reflected in the residential cities, where the houses within the ring of walls were very similar despite certain variations in size. The humble way of life of the inhabitants is also shown by the pottery; this consists of simple domestic wares with a limited number of forms.

The numerically small upper class did not have to work for their upkeep and could afford to live a trouble-free life with certain luxuries. Apart from the royal house, this included families with considerable property, which because of their economic independence also provided candidates for the high offices of state and commanders of the armed forces. The royal court and perhaps also part of the army were maintained from the levies which were collected from the farmers in the form of produce (cf. above, Chapter 9), but the king also had his own lands. As a result of this provision by the people, the king held a special position which is manifested in the building of palaces (cf. above, Chapter 6). In order to run the royal court, a certain number of officials, servants and slaves was essential. The necessary prerequisite legal conditions for the maintenance of large properties are unknown, but an increasing state of dependence seems to have been a characteristic of them. At any rate, social tension is visible during the course of the period of the monarchy which indicates the rift between the upper class and the rest of the population.

Israelite society thus consisted of only two classes. There was the rich upper class, and then there were the farmers, who possessed nothing apart from a house and a portion of land. The class difference is clearly visible in the palaces of the holders of public office, which were built according to tenets far in excess of those of domestic architecture, and this can be seen in the cities with a military or administrative function such as Megiddo and Lachish. In addition there are considerable differences in furnishing and lifestyle, as are clearly mentioned in the complaint in the Book of Amos, where the upper class is described in 6.4-6:

You who loll on beds inlaid with ivory and sprawl over your couches,
feasting on lambs from the flock and fatted calves, you who pluck the
strings of the lute and invent musical instruments like David, you who
drink wine by the bowlful and lard yourselves with the riches of oils, but
are not grieved at the ruin of Joseph.

The blatant difference between the private house and the palace clearly
shows the gap between the two social classes in Israel. Only the members
of the upper class were free of the burden of daily work and could enjoy
life to a certain degree, although they were also subject to the same rules
that determined life and to the course of historical development.

The wealth denounced by Amos was limited however to the capital
cities and the few centres of administration. The ancient Israelite residential city is by contrast extremely homogeneous in nature with minimal differences amongst the population. In ancient Israel the city thus
offered a form of security for the farming population. It reflected the
world of the farmers and thus by no means constituted a contrast as in
the case of 'town and country'. On the other hand, in its militant aspect
it demonstrated at the same time the precautions taken and demands
made by the monarchy. Thus tension did not develop between the town
and the countryside; rather the division was between the cities in the
country and the capital cities of Jerusalem and Samaria, as well as the
administrative centres. The equality that was brought about by poverty,
and which otherwise constituted an ever-present governing fact of daily
life in the city, was only absent in the palaces.

INDEXES

INDEX OF REFERENCES

INDEX OF SITES